The Mysterious  & Unknown

King Arthur

by William W. Lace

ReferencePoint Press™

San Diego, CA

For more information, contact:
ReferencePoint Press, Inc.
PO Box 27779
San Diego, CA 92198
www.ReferencePointPress.com

Picture credits:
Cover:
Maury Aaseng, 54
AP/Wide World Photos, 13, 42
Fortean Picture Archives, 6, 20, 23, 52, 57, 60, 64, 66, 69, 86, 90
North Wind, 9, 16, 27
Science Photo Library, 39

Series design and book layout:
Amy Stirnkorb

LIBRARY OF CONGRESS CATALOGING-IN-PUBLICATION DATA

Lace, William W.
   King Arthur / by William W. Lace.
      p. cm. -- (Mysterious & unknown)
Includes bibliographical references and index.
ISBN-13: 978-1-60152-033-3 (hardback)
ISBN-10: 1-60152-033-6 (hardback)

1. Arthur, King--Juvenile literature. 2. Britons--Kings and rulers--Juvenile literature. 3. Great Britain--History--To 1066--Juvenile literature. 4. Great Britain--Antiquities, Celtic--Juvenile literature. 5. Arthurian romances--Juvenile literature. I. Title.
DA152.5.A7L33 2008
942.01'4--dc22

                                                                                          2007028450

CONTENTS

FOREWORD

> **"Strange is our situation here upon earth."**
> —*Albert Einstein*

Since the beginning of recorded history, people have been perplexed, fascinated, and even terrified by events that defy explanation. While science has demystified many of these events, such as volcanic eruptions and lunar eclipses, some remain outside the scope of the provable. Do UFOs exist? Are people abducted by aliens? Can some people see into the future? These questions and many more continue to puzzle, intrigue, and confound despite the enormous advances of modern science and technology.

It is these questions, phenomena, and oddities that Reference-Point Press's *The Mysterious & Unknown* series is committed to exploring. Each volume examines historical and anecdotal evidence as well as the most recent theories surrounding the topic in debate. Fascinating primary source quotes from scientists, experts, and eyewitnesses as well as in-depth sidebars further inform the text. Full-color illustrations and photos add to each book's visual appeal. Finally, source notes, a bibliography, and a thorough index provide further reference and research support. Whether for research or the curious reader, *The Mysterious & Unknown* series is certain to satisfy those fascinated by the unexplained.

INTRODUCTION

The Grain of Truth

Just the name King Arthur swiftly and completely focuses the mind's eye on a familiar array of images. It calls forth visions of mighty castles with pennants flying from their battlements, gallant knights in shining armor riding against one another with lances as fair damsels watch breathlessly.

The tales of Arthur recall fierce battles, dramatic rescues, love triumphant, and love lost. They take us to a world of wizards, giants, and dragons—a world whose heroes are marked with chivalry, valor, wisdom, beauty, and strength, but who are also susceptible to lust, treachery, and betrayal.

It evokes other names almost equally familiar. In our imaginations we ride with Lancelot across a drawbridge or are courted by Tristram. We dance a stately pavane with Guinevere and watch Merlin's magic with amazement.

King Arthur, center, was known for taking care of his legendary knights of the Round Table. In this woodcut, King Arthur is seen watching over the knights while they sleep.

An Enduring Symbol

Arthur stands as an enduring symbol of British fortitude. His name and spirit have been invoked by leaders as remote as King Edward III in the fourteenth century or as recent as Winston Churchill during World War II in the twentieth century. Visitors can see Arthur's statue in the center of Winchester, a Round

Table in a nearby castle, and his supposed tomb at Glastonbury Abbey.

But did such a person as King Arthur ever exist? And, if he did, where does reality end and imagination begin?

The story of Arthur is like a pearl—lovely and shining, built up slowly over the centuries. Legends have added layer upon layer, each adding to the luster. A medieval monk first popularized the story as part of a "history." The Round Table came afterward and Lancelot even later.

But just as an oyster builds a pearl around a bit of grit or a speck of sand that has somehow entered its shell, the story of Arthur has, at its core, a handful of vague and tantalizing references. Have these provided a grain of truth around which the epic of Arthur has formed? Or does the entire story need to be shelved next to myths of ancient Greece and Rome? These are questions that have puzzled historians and archaeologists for centuries and whose answers—of which there are many—have yet to be confirmed.

CHAPTER 1

The Britain of Legend

The classic image of Arthur is largely the creation of Sir Thomas Malory, whose *Le Morte d'Arthur* (*The Death of Arthur*) was written in 1469–1470. In it Malory wove Welsh poems, French and German romances, and a fanciful medieval "history" into the colorful tapestry of Arthur and his knights.

Le Morte d'Arthur was originally eight separate but related books. Pioneering printer William Caxton, however, saw the possibility for a best seller when he acquired Malory's manuscript more than 10 years after the author's death in 1471. He trimmed large parts of the original, combined the eight stories into one, and used the title of the last part for the entire work.

The result is one of the most popular and enduring works in English literature, but the England described is that of Malory, not Arthur. It had long been common practice for historical figures to be portrayed in terms of the world that the writers and artists knew.

In 1405 English knights were fighting the French in the Hundred Years' War.

Malory's Arthur, therefore, becomes a fifteenth-century English knight rather than a sixth-century British warrior chieftain.

Malory's Life

The world of the English knight was one Malory knew very well. He was born in about 1405 when knights were winning glory and wealth fighting the French in the Hundred Years' War. About 50 years earlier, Edward III had founded the Order of the Garter, a select group of knights that perhaps was a conscious imitation of Arthur's Round Table.

Malory fought under the Earl of Warwick during the Hundred Years' War with France and was present with King Henry V at the siege of the cities of Rouen and Calais. He continued to serve under Warwick in the English civil conflict known as the Wars of the Roses.

Far from being the model of honor and chivalry he would later describe, Malory was charged over the years with an array of offenses including extortion, attempted murder, and rape. He served at least one prison sentence before 1462 and was in prison again when *Le Morte d'Arthur* was written. He may have died there, since he was buried at a church next to London's Newgate Prison.

His imprisonment could not have been too harsh, since he evidently had access not only to writing materials but also to numerous books, chief of which was the story of Arthur told in *The History of the Kings of Britain*, written by a monk, Geoffrey of Monmouth, more than 300 years earlier. From his cell, using these sources and with plenty of time on his hands, Malory fashioned an epic that has captured imaginations from then until now.

Arthur's Birth

Malory, echoing Geoffrey, writes that Arthur is the son of Uther Pendragon, king of Britain, and Igraine, the wife of one of Uther's dukes, Gorloris of Cornwall. When it is clear that Uther lusts after Igraine, who does not return his affections, her furious husband shuts her up in his primary castle, Tintagel, on the rocky coast of southwestern Britain, while he takes refuge in another castle nearby.

Uther follows with an army and besiegs Tintagel. Unable to take the castle by force, Uther resorts to trickery. He summons the famous magician Merlin, who turns Uther into the exact likeness of Gorloris so that he can enter the castle and make love to the unsuspecting Igraine. Merlin's condition is that he will take the child conceived by this union to be raised elsewhere.

Uther agrees, enters the castle, and—thus transformed—deceives Igraine. At about the same time, Gorloris leads a charge from his castle and is killed. Shortly afterward, Uther admits to Igraine what he has done and marries her.

When Igraine's child Arthur is born, Merlin claims him as promised and takes him to be raised by a knight, Sir Ector, who has no idea whose child he is. Two years later Uther dies, and the kingdom falls into disarray, nobles fighting among themselves for the throne.

The Sword in the Anvil

After several years Merlin has a marble block placed in the courtyard of a great church in London. The block holds an iron anvil into which is stuck a sword. Around the sword is written in letters of gold, "Whoso pulleth out this sword of this stone and anvil, is rightwise king born of all England."[1] Many try to do so, but all fail until the young Arthur succeeds, even though not realizing at the time what it means. Later, before the assembled nobility, he repeats the feat and is proclaimed king.

During Malory's time
it was customary for
authors to portray
historical figures in
terms of the world
they knew not with
historical accuracy.

Rulers of some of the lands bordering England are not ready to acknowledge Arthur, and he promptly has to fight a series of wars until finally all of Scotland and Wales are under his rule. One of his exploits is to rescue his ally King Leodegrance, and it is then that he first sees and instantly falls in love with Leodegrance's daughter Guinevere.

Being in love, however, does not keep him from having an affair with Margawse, whose husband, Arthur's enemy King Lot, sent her to spy on him. Unknown to him, Margawse is his half sister, daughter of Igraine and Gorloris. From this union comes a son, Mordred, who develops a bitter hatred for Arthur that will have dire consequences in the future.

Excalibur

In the meantime Arthur has broken his sword in a battle, and Merlin leads him to find a new one. He takes the king to a lake where Arthur sees, raised above the water, an arm holding a sword in a scabbard. A nearby damsel, the Lady of the Lake, offers Arthur the sword—Excalibur. As powerful as the sword is, the scabbard is even more so, protecting the wearer from all loss of blood. Unfortunately for Arthur, he will lose the scabbard later in the story.

Arthur then calls all his nobles to a great council at his new capital—Camelot. His kingdom now secure, Arthur decides it is time for him to marry and that Guinevere will be his queen, despite Merlin's warning that she will be unfaithful to him. Guinevere's father, Leodegrance, is so delighted that he sends not only his daughter but also the great Round Table that once belonged to Arthur's father.

The Round Table seats 150 knights and is circular so that there is no "head" and no knight takes precedence over another.

Arthur was the son of Uther Pendragon, king of Britain, and Igraine, the wife of one of Uther's dukes. When it was clear that Uther lusted after Igraine, who did not return his affections, her furious husband shut her up in his primary castle, Tintagel. Tintagel Castle is in southwestern England.

Leodegrance sends 100 knights with the table, so Arthur orders Merlin to find 50 more worthy enough to fill the rest of the seats. Only 28 can be found, however, and these are summoned to Camelot.

On the Christian religious feast day known as Pentecost, Arthur has the knights of the Round Table swear an oath that reflects the notions of chivalry at the time Malory wrote the book. The knights swear to refrain from violence against the weak, murder, cruelty, and treason. They swear always to be merciful, even toward their defeated enemies, and "always to do ladies, damosels, and gentlewomen succour [aid or rescue], upon pain of death."[2]

The Siege Perilous

After the oath, which is to be renewed every year, Merlin uses his magic to make the name of each knight appear in gold on the back of his chair. He warns, however, that three chairs are reserved. Two are for yet-unnamed knights of special merit. The third, he says, the "Siege Perilous," will one day be occupied by the purest, most perfect knight in the world, and the seat will destroy anyone else who dares sit in it. It will be that perfect knight, he adds, who will successfully seek the Holy Grail, generally portrayed as the dish or cup used by Jesus of Nazareth at the Last Supper.

Merlin will no longer directly influence Arthur's life, however. The aged magician falls hopelessly in love with Nimue, a second Lady of the Lake, following her everywhere. Over time she learns much of his magic and, when she thinks she has learned enough, shuts Merlin up in a rock "and so there for him that he came never out for all the craft he could do."[3]

Arthur also loses the services of the magic scabbard. The enchantress Morgan le Fay, daughter of Igraine and thus Arthur's half sister, plots to overthrow the king, stealing Excalibur and giving it to a knight who is to fight Arthur. Nimue, however, comes to the king's rescue. Arthur recovers Excalibur, but Morgan throws the scabbard into a lake from which it is never recovered.

The story resumes 25 years later. As Arthur holds court at Camelot, a delegation arrives from Rome. They claim that because Julius Caesar conquered Britain many years ago, it remains a Roman province and owes tribute to the emperor Lucius. After consulting his council, Arthur replies that instead of acknowledging Lucius, he himself has a claim to the Roman Empire since a former emperor, Constantine, had been born to a British mother.

War Against Rome

Arthur therefore amasses an army, which by now includes the young and powerful Sir Lancelot, and sets off for the European mainland, landing in Flanders. He eventually encounters Lucius's army in the Vale of Sessoine and, fighting the emperor hand-to-hand, "smote him again with Excalibur that it cleft his head, from the summit of his head, and stinted not till it came to his breast. And then the emperor fell down dead and there ended his life."[4]

With Lucius and more than 100,000 of his soldiers dead, Arthur proceeds on a march through Europe, finally arriving in Rome, where he is crowned emperor by the pope. When his knights begs him to take them back to Britain, he agrees, setting up governments in the lands he has conquered and then sailing back home, where he is royally welcomed by Queen Guinevere.

At this point Arthur becomes almost a minor character in Malory's story. Instead, large segments—more than half the book— are devoted to the exploits of other members of the court. Chief among these are the stories of Lancelot and Guinevere, Sir Tristram, Sir Gareth, and the search for the Holy Grail.

Arthur is given his legendary sword, Excalibur, by the Lady of the Lake.

Lancelot and Guinevere

After Arthur returns from Rome, Lancelot is acknowledged as the foremost knight of the Round Table. Guinevere "had him in great favour above all other knights, and in certain he loved the queen again above all other ladies and damosels of his life."[5] Unfortunately, their affection for one another soon develops into a passion.

Both are unwilling, for a time at least, to deceive Arthur, so Lancelot sets out to find adventures. Of the many recounted, the most important occur when Lancelot meets King Pelles, a descendant of Joseph of Arimathea, the man who supposedly brought the Holy Grail from Palestine to Britain. Pelles wants Lancelot to impregnate his daughter Elaine so as to produce the knight who will eventually find the Grail. To do so, he tricks Lancelot into drinking a love potion that makes Elaine look like Guinevere. His plan works and leads to the eventual birth of Sir Galahad.

Tristram and Isolde

Interposed between the stories of Lancelot and Guinevere are those of Tristram and Gareth. Tristram, nephew of King Mark of Cornwall, is sent to Ireland by his uncle to fetch the king's prospective bride, Isolde. On the return trip, however, the pair accidentally drink a magic potion and fall in love.

Later, after Mark and Isolde are married, she and Tristram are discovered committing adultery. Mark banishes Tristram and has Isolde locked up. Tristram winds up in Arthur's court and is so valorous there that Arthur forces Mark to rescind the exile. Tristram returns to Cornwall, is treacherously imprisoned by Mark, but escapes with Isolde.

Malory ends his tale of Tristram and Isolde with the lovers living happily in Lancelot's castle. He admits, however, that the story has not ended, writing, "Here endeth the second book of Sir Tristram that was drawn out of French into English. But here is no rehersal of the third book."[6] In fact, the various French versions on which Malory drew end in the lovers' deaths.

Gareth and Linet

Another story given a happy ending is that of Sir Gareth, youngest son of Lot and Margawse and brother of three of Arthur's most famous knights—Gawaine, Gaheris, and Agravaine. He comes to Arthur's court and—not revealing his identity and unrecognized by his brothers—asks for food and lodging for a year. Gareth is scornfully nicknamed "Beaumains," or fair hands, and sent to work in the kitchen.

When the damsel Linet arrives to ask Arthur to furnish a knight to rescue her sister Dame Lionesse from captivity, Gareth volunteers and, knighted by Lancelot as Sir Beaumains, sets out with Linet, who is furious to have only a kitchen boy for a champion. Gareth, however, proves his worth, overcoming every adversary and marrying the rescued lady.

Quest for the Grail

Malory's tale more or less comes together again in the story of the Sangreal, or Holy Grail. Lancelot's son Galahad, now of age, is led to Camelot by a mysterious old man and seated in the Siege Perilous. Arthur takes this as a sign that there should be a quest for the Holy Grail.

Later, as the knights are eating, the Grail, covered by a white cloth, appears in a ray of light and then disappears. First Gawaine then all the knights of the Round Table vow to go in search of the Grail. They leave the next day, much to the sorrow of Arthur, who knows the Round Table will never be the same.

Lancelot, of course, is one of those on the quest, but it is revealed to him that he is unworthy to succeed because of his adultery with Guinevere. At great length Galahad, accompanied by two other knights, Perceval and Bors, discovers the Grail, covered this time by a red cloth, on a magic boat and sails to the mystical land of Sarras, where he is made king.

After a year Joseph of Arimathea appears to Galahad and reveals the Grail to him in its full glory. Galahad then dies and Bors and Perceval see "a great multitude of angels bare his soul up to heaven" after which an enormous hand "came right to the Vessel, and took it and the spear, and so bare it up to heaven."[7] Perceval dies shortly afterward, but Bors makes his way back to Camelot, where he told his story.

The Fatal Affair

Malory then returns to perhaps the best-known part of the Arthurian saga—the love triangle of Arthur, Guinevere, and Lancelot. Guinevere and Lancelot become less cautious about their relationship to the point where everyone except Arthur knows about it. This includes Arthur's nephew/son, Mordred, still nursing his hatred for the king.

One night Mordred and his brother Agravaine burst in on Lancelot and Guinevere. Mordred calls Lancelot a traitor and Lancelot, in making his escape, kills Agravaine. Mordred reveals the queen's behavior to Arthur, who sorrowfully orders her to be burned at the stake.

Lancelot rides to her rescue and takes her off to his castle. Arthur responds by rallying his knights to besiege Lancelot's

*The dying
King Arthur
asked one of
his knights to
put his sword
back into the
lake. When the
knight finally
obeys this order,
a hand reaches
up and takes the
sword under
the water.*

castle. The pope intervened, ordering Lancelot to return Guinevere to Arthur. Lancelot obeys and withdraws to France, taking 100 knights with him.

Arthur is determined to punish Lancelot and sails to France with an army, having left England—and Guinevere—in Mordred's hands, little realizing how much Mordred hates him. Arthur besieges Lancelot's castle, but before the conflict is resolved he hears that Mordred is planning to be crowned king and to marry Guinevere, claiming that Arthur has been killed.

The Last Battle

Arthur rushes home with his army and meets Mordred in three battles. At the climax of the third battle, Arthur runs a spear through Mordred's body, but Mordred, knowing the wound is fatal, is able to pull himself up the spear to the point where he can deliver a two-handed sword blow that pierces Arthur's helmet into his skull.

After one of Arthur's knights, Bedivere, moves him to safety, Arthur orders him to take the sword Excalibur and throw it into the nearby sea. Twice Bedivere hides the sword, claiming to have done Arthur's bidding. Each time, when Arthur asks him what has happened, his answers are not what Arthur knows is supposed to occur. Bedivere finally obeys, and a hand reaches up out of the sea, catches Excalibur, flourishes it three times, then withdraws under the surface.

Bedivere then carries Arthur to the sea, whereupon a barge appears bearing three queens, including Morgan le Fay, and their ladies. They take Arthur onto the barge, and as it departs into the mist Arthur says he is being taken to the Vale of Avalon to be healed.

The Final Battle

S ir Thomas Malory in *Le Morte d'Arthur* writes that the final battle between King Arthur and Mordred takes place after Arthur learns that Mordred is planning both to take his throne and to marry Queen Guinevere. He relates that at the end of a long day of fighting, the two meet in hand-to-hand combat:

> Then the king gat his spear in both his hands, and ran toward Sir Mordred, crying: Traitor, now is thy death-day come. And when Sir Mordred heard Sir Arthur, he ran toward him with his sword drawn in his hand. And there King Arthur smote Sir Mordred under the shield, with a foin [thrust] of his spear, throughout the body, more than

Continued on page 24

In this drawing Arthur has been fatally wounded and is being taken on a barge to be healed. The end of the tale leaves much room for questioning Arthur's supposed death.

Continued from page 22

a fathom. And when Sir Mordred felt that he had his death wound he thrust himself with the might that he had up to the bur [hilt] of King Arthur's spear. And right so he smote his father Arthur, with his sword holden in both his hands, on the side of the head, that the sword pierced the helmet and the brain-pan, and therewithal Sir Mordred fell stark dead to the earth; and the noble Arthur fell in a swoon to the earth, and there he swooned ofttimes. And Sir Lucan the Butler and Sir Bedivere ofttimes heaved him up. And so weakly they led him betwixt them both, to a little chapel not far from the seaside.

Bedivere wanders through the night and the next day arrives at Glastonbury Abbey. There he finds a hermit who says three queens have brought a dead body and requested him to bury it. Bedivere assumes the body is Arthur's.

On hearing of Arthur's death Guinevere becomes a nun, and Lancelot later becomes a monk in France, returning six years later only to bury Guinevere's body next to Arthur's at Glastonbury Abbey, after which Lancelot soon dies.

"The King That Will Be"

Was Arthur really dead? Malory leaves plenty of room for doubt. The body at Glastonbury is never positively identified as Arthur's, and Malory writes that "men say that he shall come again" and that "there is written upon his tomb this verse: *Hic jacet Arthurus, Rex quondam, Rexque futurus* [Here lies Arthur, the king that was and the king that will be]."[8]

Such is the picture of Arthur drawn by Malory and copied by others through the centuries. It clearly cannot be taken as history—there was no Roman emperor named Lucius, for instance, and certainly no British conquest of Rome. Rather, it is a romance—dibs and daubs of ancient histories and legends spread on a distinctly fifteenth-century canvas.

The real King Arthur—if, indeed, such a person ever was—lived almost 1,000 years earlier. And Arthur's Britain and its history were far different from that of Malory's.

CHAPTER 2

The Britain of History

The Britain in which King Arthur would have lived bore little resemblance to the fanciful picture portrayed in later centuries. There were no great stone castles, no suits of shining armor, no great tournaments at which knights strove to prove themselves against one another. There was not even an England. That would come later, the name taken from invaders against whom Arthur would have fought.

Instead, Britain in the 400s and 500s was a rapidly fading shadow of the great Roman Empire. To Arthur and his contemporaries fell the task of keeping the flickering light of classical civilization burning in the face of barbarian hordes. They would succeed—for a time—but Britain would eventually be conquered and fall into what is known as the Dark Ages.

In 330, the great Roman Emperor Constantine, moved the Roman capitol to Byzantium, which he renamed Constantinople. He was born in Britain, the son of a Roman general and a British mother.

Britain was first drawn into the Roman orbit as a result of raids starting in 55 B.C. by Julius Caesar and his legions. The people they fought were Celts, descendants of tribes that had moved into Britain 500 years earlier, pushing the earlier natives west into what is now Wales and north into what is now Scotland.

The Roman Conquest
The raids became a full-scale invasion in A.D. 43 when 4 Roman legions—about 25,000 veteran troops plus auxiliaries—crossed

the narrow sea and began a slow but sure advance across the island. It was not an easy conquest. In about 61, Boudicca, queen of the Iceni, led a revolt in which an estimated 70,000 Roman soldiers and settlers were killed and the new commercial capital of London was burned to the ground.

The revolt was crushed, Boudicca committed suicide, and the conquest of Britain continued. By the year 80 the Romans controlled every area except for Scotland, which they considered not worth the trouble. To help prevent raids from Scotland, however, they built Hadrian's Wall, a fortification across the northern frontier.

By 300 most of the island was peaceful. Trade with the European continent flourished, and commerce moved briskly along a network of roadways. Prosperous Britons, now officially Roman citizens, took an active part in the affairs of the empire. One of the greatest Roman emperors, Constantine I, was born in Britain, son of a Roman general and his British wife.

It was Constantine, ironically, who took the step that would eventually lead to much of Britain's trouble. In 330, once his position as emperor was solidified, he moved his capital eastward to Byzantium, which he renamed Constantinople. With the royal court and much of the nobility removed, Rome began to decline. Raids on outlying provinces became more frequent, and the once invincible legions were hard put to prevent them.

Britons Under Attack

Britain suffered its share of such raids. As Roman soldiers were withdrawn to defend regions closer to home, the so-called barbarians became bolder. The Picts attacked from the north. The Irish, whom the Romans had never attempted to conquer, raided from the west. And a new enemy, known collectively by the Romano-Britons as the *Saxones*, began increasing their hit-and-run raids from the European mainland.

The *Saxones* were actually made up of three Germanic tribes— the Saxons, Angles (from whom the name England would be taken), and Jutes—who later became known as the Anglo-Saxons. Their migration westward was part of a process begun when the fierce Huns stormed out of central Asia, forcing other tribes out of their native areas and into Roman territory. At the same time the Anglo-Saxons were making forays to Britain, the Visigoths, Franks, and Vandals were putting pressure on Gaul (present-day France) and northern Italy.

To counter the Anglo-Saxon raids, the Romano-Britons built a chain of tower forts along the southeastern shore. These were commanded by an official called the Count of the Saxon Shore, who could call out troops to fight off any landing attempt.

The system of defenses was put to its most severe test in 367 when the Irish, Picts, and Anglo-Saxons mounted what appeared to be a planned combined assault. The Roman troops stationed in Britain were unable to deal with the situation, and it took reinforcements from Gaul and three years of fighting before peace could be restored.

In some ways the British—or at least their Roman governors— were their own worst enemies. First Magnus Maximus in 287 and then Constantine III in 407 used their power base in Britain to declare themselves emperor. Both crossed into Gaul, taking troops with them and intending to make their claim good by force, but both were defeated. In addition, Rome was forced to recall additional soldiers to defend the city itself from a Visigoth attack.

Britain Defenseless

The end result was to strip Britain bare of Roman legions, leaving the Romanized British natives almost defenseless, and the barbarian incursions increased. Desperate, the British leaders wrote to Rome for help. In 410 the besieged emperor of Rome, Honarius, replied that—in effect—they were on their own.

But the British, having lived for centuries under the protection of Roman legions, were not equal to the task. The monk Gildas, writing in about 545, quotes a later appeal for help: "To Aetius, now consul for the third time: the groans of the Britons. . . . The barbarians drive us to the sea; the sea throws us back on the barbarians: thus two modes of death await us, we are either slain or drowned."[9]

Finally, in desperation, the British king Vortigern had an idea. If the British could not defeat the barbarians, perhaps they could hire other barbarians to do it for them.

The eighth-century monk Bede, in his *Ecclesiastical History of the English Nation* writtes that in 449 three shiploads of Angles arrived at Vortigern's invitation and were given land in the southeastern part of the island on the condition they would fight the Picts. They were successful but quickly saw that much more was theirs for the taking. According to Bede, they sent messengers back to their homeland, and when the Angles there heard about "the fertility of the country, and the cowardice of the Britons, a more considerable fleet was quickly sent over, bringing a still greater number of men, which, being added to the former, made up an invincible army."[10]

The Mercenaries Revolt

Accordingly, writes Bede, not only the Angles but also hosts of Saxons and Jutes set sail for Britain, commanded by the brothers Hengist and Horsa. Like those who had preceded them, they first fought Vortigern's enemies, but then they turned on those who had invited them. Bede writes that they initially demanded more supplies, and when the demand was not met they proceeded to "break the confederacy, and ravage all the island."[11]

Bede's account tallies with that of Gildas, most of whose *Concerning the Ruin of Britain* is a bitter denunciation of weak British rulers whose policy led to the invasion. They were, he writes,

> "So blinded, that, as a protection to their country, they sealed its doom by inviting in among them (like wolves into the sheep-fold), the fierce and impious Saxons."
> —Gildas, a sixth-century monk writes about weak British rule.

> so blinded, that, as a protection to their country, they sealed its doom by inviting in among them (like wolves into the sheep-fold), the fierce and impious Saxons, a race hateful both to God and men, to repel the invasions of the northern nations. Nothing was ever so pernicious to our country, nothing was ever so unlucky. What palpable darkness must have enveloped their minds—darkness desperate and cruel! Those very people whom, when absent, they dreaded more than death itself, were invited to reside, as one may say, under the selfsame roof.[12]

At first the invaders seem to have been unstoppable. The *Anglo-Saxon Chronicle*, begun in the 800s, records major Anglo-Saxon victories in 455 and 456, stating that after the second battle "the Britons gave up [the county of] Kent, and in great fear fled to London."[13]

Tale of Destruction

Gildas is much more descriptive:

> All the columns were leveled with the ground by the frequent strokes of the battering-ram, all the husbandmen routed, together with their bishops, priests, and people, whilst the sword gleamed, and the flames crackled around them on every side. . . . In the midst of the streets lay the tops of lofty towers, tumbled to the ground, stones of high walls, holy altars, fragments of human bodies, covered with livid clots of coagulated blood, looking as if they had been squeezed together in a press. . . . Some, therefore, of the miserable remnant, being taken in the mountains, were murdered in great numbers; others, constrained by famine, came and yielded themselves to be slaves for ever to their foes, running the risk of being instantly slain, which truly was the greatest favour that could be offered them: some others passed beyond the seas with loud lamentations.[14]

Most of those who chose to leave Britain sailed from the southwestern areas of Devon and Cornwall across the English Channel. They did so in such numbers that the area the Romans called Armorica became known as Brittany and was an independent nation speaking a Celtic language until it was later absorbed into France.

Ambrosius Aurelianus

The *Anglo-Saxon Chronicle* refers to only one additional battle over the next 17 years and does not claim an outright Anglo-Saxon victory. Gildas, however, writes of a British resurgence under a new leader, Ambrosius Aurelianus. He is not described as a king but as a "modest man" whose parents had been "adorned with the purple," perhaps meaning that his father had been a high-ranking official.[15]

Rallying around Ambrosius, the British seem to have halted the Anglo-Saxon advance. Perhaps they took advantage of some event that drew many of the invaders back to their homeland since Gildas says Ambrosius was able to succeed "when these most cruel robbers were returned home." Warfare continued for years on end, during which, Gildas writes, "sometimes our countrymen, sometimes the enemy, won the field."[16]

This warfare between the British and Anglo-Saxons was very different from the conflict described by Malory. For one thing, plate armor such as the knights were portrayed as wearing would not come into use until the 1200s. Roman legionnaires had worn cuirasses, or plates, covering the upper body. These were normally made of leather, although those of officers could be bronze or iron.

Mail Armor

Arthur and his fellow British leaders might have worn metal cuirasses, but it is far more likely that they wore chain mail. This armor was constructed of interlocking iron rings fashioned into a protective garment—either a byrnie (waist length), hauberk (knee length), or haubergeon (mid-thigh length). The warrior chief also would probably have worn a mail coif, or head covering, but metal helmets would have been rare.

Mail armor, however, was time-consuming to make—as many as 40,000 rings composed a hauberk—and thus was very expensive. Ordinary soldiers would have worn—if they wore armor at all—a thick leather jerkin, or short jacket.

While mail could protect the wearer against sword cuts or spear thrusts, it did nothing to cushion the blow. Therefore, body mail was usually worn over a padded garment of some kind.

The invading Anglo-Saxons, judging from graves that have been excavated, were even less protected. Mail armor was almost unknown, and the large majority of warriors went into battle with nothing more than a spear and shield. The shields were not the elaborate, highly decorated affairs sometimes pictured but round pieces of leather-covered wood about three feet in diameter.

Weapons and Cavalry

Both sides used swords, but instead of the long swords often pictured they were about three feet long at most, sharpened on both sides and used more for slashing than stabbing. Stabbing was done with lances or pikes, with shorter spears such as javelins used for throwing.

Horses had been used for war in Britain for centuries. Julius Caesar had fought off cavalry charges, and the Anglo-Saxons had to do the same. Archaeologists have found very little evidence, however, that the Anglo-Saxons were horsemen. This would have given the British forces a decided advantage in mobility, against which the Anglo-Saxons would have needed numerical superiority.

Thus equipped, the British fought to keep their homeland, and the Anglo-Saxons fought to take it. At least one historical document indicates that for a time the British were successful. In 468 they appeared to be strong enough for the emperor in Rome to request their help.

By this time the Roman Empire had split into eastern and western divisions. Jordanes, a historian writing in the Eastern Roman Empire at about the same time as Gildas, relates that when the Visigoths threatened to take over Gaul, "the emperor Anthemius heard of it and asked the Britons for aid. Their king Riotimus came with twelve thousand men into the state of the Bituriges by way of Ocean, and was received as he disembarked from his ships."[17]

Riotimus remains something of a mystery. Gildas does not refer to him, and some historians think Jordanes meant Britanny instead of Britain, even though he specified that help came "by ocean." Regardless, Riotimus was eventually defeated by the Visigoths and retreated. Nothing more is heard of him, but if he was indeed a British king, he might have had some kind of link to Arthur.

The Great Victory

Eventually the struggle between the Britons and Anglo-Saxons reached a climax when the invaders were soundly defeated in the battle Gildas calls Mons Badonicus, variously translated as Badon, Mount Bath, or Baddesdownhill. No one is sure exactly where this momentous battle took place, although a hill northeast of the modern city of Bath or a hill at Badbury more to the east have been suggested as possible sites.

The date is also uncertain, but regardless of when or where it was, the Battle of Badon seems to have been a resounding victory for the Britons. Whom their leader was, however, is unknown. Gildas does not say. It is unlikely that Ambrosius was still in command. He is known to have fought a battle in 437 and

Putting Arthur on the Map

King Arthur's fame is such that places throughout Britain have been quick to claim him as their own, or at least to point to local landmarks claimed to be associated with him. The most famous, and the greatest tourist attraction, is Glastonbury Abbey, the site of what supposedly was Arthur's grave but which many experts suspect was a fraud.

The legendary ruler is also associated with a hill in Edinburg called Arthur's Seat, Arthur's Knot

would probably have been well into his 70s, even if the battle had been fought in 483 as many believe. Some have speculated that it was Arthur, his successor, who won the great victory.

That victory ushered in a time of relative peace, at least with the Anglo-Saxons. Gildas describes the "present prosperity" but adds that the country is still troubled, "our foreign wars having ceased, but our civil troubles still remaining."[18] By the time he was writing, British unity had collapsed, and petty rulers fought among themselves.

(earthworks near Stirling, Scotland), Arthur's Oven (a stone building, now destroyed, also near Stirling), and numerous stone circles named Arthur's Quoit, after the rings used in a game similar to horseshoes.

One of the most unusual sites is described in *The Marvels of Britain*, an appendix to the Welsh monk Nennius's *Historia Brittonum*. It is a cairn, or heap of stones, supposedly the burial place of Arthur's dog, Cabal. Nennius, or whoever may have attached the *Marvels* to his history, wrote that atop the cairn was one stone with the footprint of a dog. It was said that no matter how many times this stone was carried away as a souvenir, it would miraculously reappear the next morning.

Also by this time the Anglo-Saxons, having presumably been confined in the east and southeast, resumed their conquest. The *Anglo-Saxon Chronicle* lists several victories over the Britons from 552 through 584, after which little is heard about them.

The Britons who survived took refuge far to the west in Wales or Cornwall. They took with them the memory of how they had risen up and thrown back a barbarian invasion. They kept this memory alive in stories, poems, and songs, and out of these— perhaps real, perhaps not—came the figure of Arthur.

CHAPTER 3

The Historical Arthur

Compiling a "biography" of Arthur is like trying to solve a jigsaw puzzle using pieces from several related, yet very different, boxes. The pieces—snippets of poetry, an offhand mention in a letter, chronicles that give different names, times, and places for the same people or events—do not mesh very well. Sometimes one has to cut corners to make them fit, and when finally finished, the resulting picture is still extremely indistinct.

Not a single fact about Arthur—date and place of birth, parentage, military career, death—is historically verifiable. And yet there are enough clues to allow a vague outline to emerge from legend.

The earliest clue as to when Arthur lived comes from the *Historia Brittonum* compiled by the Welsh monk Nennius in about 830. Nennius makes no claim to scholarship, saying only that he "heaped together all that I found"[19] from various Roman, British, Saxon, and Irish sources.

In one passage he writes that Arthur fought against the Saxons shortly after the death of their leader Hengist. Since the *Anglo-Saxon Chronicle* puts Hengist's death in 488, this must have been about the start of Arthur's exploits as a military leader.

"Leader of Battles"

Arthur, Nennius writes, was at that time a "leader of battles."[20] Since multiple sources indicate—without specifically saying so—that Arthur succeeded Ambrosius, he would have been a seasoned warrior, perhaps a few years over 20 in an age when boys were considered to have become men at about age 15. This, then, would put the year of Arthur's birth at about 465.

As to his birthplace, Geoffrey of Monmouth places it at Tintagel, a rocky outcropping on the northern coast of Cornwall. Archaeological research has shown that this might be possible.

Geoffrey's vivid description of the site indicates that he probably had visited it, but the castle whose ruins can be seen there dates from the 1230s, long after Geoffrey. It was built by Richard, Earl of Cornwall, an illegitimate son of King Henry III, who may have been trying to link himself with the Arthur legend through the popularity of Geoffrey's history.

There may have been an earlier castle, this one built by a previous Earl of Cornwall at about the same time Geoffrey was writing. This earl, Reginald, was the brother of Geoffrey's patron, the Earl of Gloucester. Some have suggested that Geoffrey placed Arthur at Tintagel to please his benefactor.

Archaeology at Tintagel

Archaeology on the site in the 1930s revealed much earlier structures that until fairly recently had been thought to be the remains

Tintagel Head, on which the remains of Tintagel Castle exist, is considered an archaeological site. New discoveries were made there as recently as 1998.

of a small community of monks. What was puzzling, however, was that fragments of high-quality pottery of Mediterranean origin were found—not the kind likely used by poor monks.

In 1983, however, a fire revealed the foundations of these buildings as Roman in style, indicating that the site had been occupied earlier, even before Arthur's time. It seems to have been a commercial site, which would explain the pottery.

A possible connection with Arthur himself was found in 1998

in the form of a piece of inscribed slate that, because of the level at which it was discovered, has been firmly dated in the 500s. The fragmentary Latin inscription involves a person named Artognou. Whether the stone is from a memorial to Artognou or whether Artognou could possibly be King Arthur is unknown.

Although he may or may not have been born at Tintagel, most authorities consider it likely that Arthur came from the general area of southwestern Britain. There is another school of thought, however, that says he came from the far north and was not even British.

Y Gododdin

One of the oldest references to Arthur is found in the Welsh poem *Y Gododdin*, written in the early 600s by a bard named Aneurin. It relates the exploits of a group of warriors who were probably from the kingdom of the Votadini, a Pictish people in what is now Scotland who were allied with the British against the Anglo-Saxons. It describes one particular hero, saying that while he fought bravely and killed many enemies, "he was no Arthur."[21] This reference, coming far in advance of any mention of Tintagel, has led some experts to believe that Arthur came from the north instead of the west.

Arthur's name provides clues as to what his background may have been, but some of them lead in different directions. The Latin form of Arthur is Artorius, a name known to have existed in Britain in the person of an army commander in the late 100s. This suggests that Arthur may have been from the same kind of family as that of Ambrosius, either descended from Roman officials or from thoroughly Romanized Britons. The likelihood of such a background increases when one considers that Arthur was generally recognized as Ambrosius's successor.

This piece of inscribed slate, discovered in 1998 on Tintagel Head, was dated in the 500s and perhaps inscribed with Arthur's name.

The Nickname Issue

On the other hand, some historians have suggested that one way of explaining why the name of so important a person as Arthur has not survived on any official document or letter is that it was not his name at all, but a nickname. The Celtic word for "bear" is *arth*, and speculation is that Arthur may have acquired such a name because of his might in battle.

Indeed, there are multiple references that support this view. Gildas referred to a contemporary of Arthur, Cuneglasus, as having been "the bear's charioteer."[22] And a thirteenth-century commentary on Nennius describes Arthur as "cruel from his boyhood, a horrible son, a horrible bear, an iron hammer."[23] Another twist to the bear idea, one posed by Graham Phillips and Martin Keatman in their book *King Arthur: The True Story*, is that both the Celtic word for bear and its Latin equivalent, *ursus*, were combined to produce Arthursus.

In fact, both versions of Arthur's name could be correct. The nickname could have come into use because his real name, Artorius, sounded so much like the word for bear, which seemed to match his ferocity.

The comment on Nennius, however, raises another issue—that of Arthur's personality and character. The comment is not the only one that portrays Arthur as far removed from the brave, wise, chivalrous hero of Geoffrey and Malory.

The Triads

These occur mainly in the Triads, a collection of Welsh folk stories compiled in the Middle Ages and so called because they were grouped into threes. One charges Arthur with removing a magical talisman or charm against invasion and thus directly bringing about the ultimate Anglo-Saxon victory. Another calls him a curse on the land, and yet others portray him in such undignified roles as a frivolous bard and a pig thief. Other parts of the Triads, however, give Arthur his traditional positive virtues.

Arthur's Funeral Ode

The Welsh *Marwnad [Funeral Ode] Uthyr Pendrag-on* was long thought to have been written to honor King Arthur's father, Uther. *Uthyr*, however, can be translated as "wonderful" instead of as a proper name. The specific mention of Arthur indicates that it might have been written for Arthur. This excerpt is found in Rodney Castleden's *King Arthur: The Truth Behind the Legend*.

> The longing and lamentation of the mul-titude
> Are unceasing throughout the host. . . .

Indeed, these could safely be called Christian virtues since it is all but certain that Arthur was of that religion. Christianity, however, was by no means a given in Dark Ages Britain. It had spread into the island shortly after the Roman invasion, but paganism was still widespread in many areas in Arthur's time, especially

All around appears the rule of order at the
head of the feast.
They seek to dress the head of the feast
with black.
They unendingly shed blood among the
war-bands,
Longing for you to defend them and give
them succor [aid].
At the vanishing of Caesar's kinsman
They will shout in blood and anger. . . .
They crave with longing for a portion of
your cause
And for the refuge and manliness of Ar-
thur.

Rodney Castleden, *King Arthur: The Truth Behind the Legend.* London: Routledge,
2000.

in the north and far west. Nennius, however, writes that Arthur
went into one battle with "the image of the Holy Virgin, mother
of God, upon his shoulders,"[24] probably meaning he had a picture of Mary on his shield.

Depictions of Arthur as vengeful and ruthless, however, could well be correct despite his Christianity. A ruler or military leader in this era had to be harsh to be successful or even to survive. Arthur could hardly have been expected to exhibit the kind of mercy pictured by Malory. Instead, he would have been harsh, even in treatment of defeated enemies, in order to set an example for those who remained.

As for the tales that picture Arthur as a fool, thief, or enemy of his own people, he would have had numerous enemies other than the invading Anglo-Saxons. In reaching a position of overall command, he would have faced rival leaders or chiefs in whose courts or from whose poets such stories might have sprung.

King or General?

But what kind of overall command would Arthur have had? Was he a king or some kind of emperor to whom other kings owed allegiance? Or was he not a king at all but a warlord or general? Nennius never refers to him as a king, writing instead that he fought "with all the kings and military force of Britain" and that "there were many more noble than himself."[25] Indeed, Britain was not considered a country in the modern sense, with a king. Instead, it was home to several small tribal units, each headed by a king.

Another translation of Nennius has him calling Arthur a "leader of battles,"[26] or *dux bellorum* in Latin. While *dux* is the word from which the title of duke is derived, dukes did not exist in the same sense in Arthur's time as in the Later Middle Ages.

These passages along with another from Nennius referring to "Arthur the soldier"[27] suggest that far from being a king with lesser kings under his rule, he was a military commander. He would have had to be a very gifted and successful general indeed to have kings put themselves and their forces at his command.

Jack Lindsay writes in *Arthur and His Times* that Arthur does not appear in any of the genealogies of the various royal houses and adds, "On the whole it is best to consider Arthur a brilliant general who won his reputation under Ambrosius and who was entrusted with an overriding commission during a period of pressing danger from the Saxon invaders."[28]

The idea that Arthur had been a king does not seem to have taken hold—or at least made its way into literature—until about 500 years after his death. A priest in Britanny named William wrote an account of the legendary St. Goeznovius in about 1019. In it he relates the Saxon invasion of Britain and writes that "their pride was checked for a while through the great Arthur, king of the Britons."[29]

Arthur's kingship, however, probably originated earlier. William, in fact, writes that he has obtained information from a book, the *Ystoria Britanica*, no trace of which has ever been found. Geoffrey, more than a century later, made much the same claim, writing that he used "a certain very ancient book written in the British language."[30] As with William, no one has been able to discover what book that could have been. Some historians speculate that William and Geoffrey used a common source, now lost, or that Geoffrey used William as a source, particularly since the narratives have striking parallels such as Arthur's invasion of Gaul.

Arthur's Capital

If Arthur was a king, where was his court? Welsh legends put it at Celliwig, a spot in Cornwall said to be not far from Tintagel. Such a site has not been discovered, and experts are unsure as to where it might have been.

Caerleon, a village in southeastern Wales, is another candidate. It served as a major Roman military center for more than 200 years, and it is here than Geoffrey placed Arthur's court. Later medieval writers such as Wace and Layamon agreed with Geoffrey, and Malory had Arthur crowned at "Carilon."

Camelot, however, is the name most universally associated with having been Arthur's capital and the place where the Round Table was housed. It was first used by the French poet Chrétien de Troyes in about 1180. He may have been referring to Camulodunum, the Roman name for Colchester, but that city is too far to the east to have been used by Arthur.

A much more likely candidate, and one strengthened by archaeology, is Cadbury Castle, a Dark Ages hill fort in southeastern England. The names of two nearby villages—Queen Camel and West Camel—serve as clues, and old folktales claim that there is a hidden cave in the hill in which Arthur is sleeping, ready to emerge in time of trouble.

Such tales prompted John Leland, official historian to King Henry VIII, to write in the 1500s, "At the very south ende of the chirch of South-Cadbyri standith Camallate, sumtyme a famose toun or castelle, upon a very torre or hill. . . . The people can telle nothing ther but that they have hard say that Arture much restorid to Camalat."[31]

Unearthing the Castle

Archaeologist Leslie Alcock's work on Cadbury Castle in the 1960s revealed remnants of a large fortified enclosure similar to those of Arthur's time period. It was constructed primarily of wood—certainly nothing like the massive stone structures usually pictured as Camelot—but was clearly a major center.

The problem was that nothing found there could be connected with anyone named Arthur. It could, for instance, have been the headquarters of another ruler, perhaps Vortigern.

Cadbury Castle's location, however, would have been perfect for Arthur's military exploits. It was next to Roman roads over which his mounted warriors could cover large amounts of territory—and the battles that Arthur is supposed to have fought cover a large territory, indeed.

Nennius writes that Arthur "was twelve times chosen their [the Britons'] commander, and was as often conqueror." He goes on to list the 12 battles: at the mouth of the River Gleni; the next four near the river "Duglas, in the region Linuis;" near the River Bassas; in the Celidon [Calidonian] wood; near Gurnion castle; at the "City of Legion"[32] [Caerleon]; near the River Trat Treuroit; on Mount Breguoin; and finally the Battle of Badon.

Locating the Sites

Generations of historians and archaeologists have pored over British place-names, trying to pinpoint the sites of these battles. Unfortunately, there are multiple candidates for almost every one. There is a Glen River in Lincolnshire in eastern England, however, and, although there are many Duglas or Douglas rivers in Britain, the "region Linuis" could well be the Lindsey area near Lincolnshire. All five of these battles, then, would have been fought in the same general area, probably against the Angles.

On the other hand, those who think Arthur came from the north point to the Glen River in Northumberland near the present England-Scotland border and the River Dunglas in southern Scotland. Furthermore, they say, Bassas refers to Bass Rock in the Firth of Forth northeast of Edinburg, Scotland, although others argue for Basachurch far to the southeast, close to Wales.

At least one of the battles, however, was probably fought in the north. Caledonia was the Roman name for present-day Scotland, and the battle site is presumed to be there. Some writers, however, theorize that Celidon could come from the Welsh words for "grove" and "fort" and that that battle was fought there. City of Legions (Caerleon) is most likely, as Nennius writes, but that phrase is also used in some references to the city of Chester.

Badon

By far the most important of these battles, and the only one mentioned by most other sources, is Badon, assumed by most authorities to have taken place near the present city of Bath in southeast England. As with the other battles, other sites are proposed, but the key question about Badon is not where, but when. Fixing the date of the battle would go a long way in determining who Arthur was.

Unfortunately, dating Badon is not easy. Gildas writes that it occurred "forty-four years and one month after the landing of the Saxons,"[33] which would put it in the year 493 if the invasion date of 449 is correct. He may have been referring, however, not to the original mercenaries invited by Vortigern but to a much larger migration by the Saxons in about 477, which would date Badon at about 521. On the other hand, Gildas adds the words "and also the time of my own nativity,"[34] which presents no problem if he meant that the battle was fought in the year he was born. Some have translated this passage, however, to say that Gildas was 44 years old when he was writing and that the battle had occurred 44 years before. Since he very likely wrote his history about 550, this would put the battle at 506.

Fortunately, another source exists—the *Annals of Wales*, or *Annales Cambriae*, a chronology compiled in Wales about the year 955. Although many of the dates given are suspect, many others can be verified. The entry for 516 is for "The Battle of Badon, in which Arthur carried the Cross of our Lord Jesus Christ for three days and three nights on his shoulders and the Britons were the victors."[35] Such a date would be very close to the 521 interpretation of Gildas.

After his great victory at Badon, however, Arthur is supposed to have fought at least one more great battle. The *Annals of Wales* says that in 537 was fought "the battle of Camlannn, in which Arthur and Medraut fell: and there was plague in Britain and Ireland."[36] The site of the battle, as with so many others, is the source of intense speculation. Most candidates are in southeast England or in Wales, but one possibility is Camelon in Scotland.

Medraut is the Welsh equivalent of Mordred, Arthur's son/nephew who in Geoffrey and Malory's versions leads a rebellion that causes the final battle. The *Annals* entry, however, does not say that Arthur and Mordred were related or that they fought one another. Indeed, they may even have been on the same side, except that references to Medraut in the Welsh Triads make it seem as if he were Arthur's rival. One such passage describes an incident in which Medraut "came to Arthur's court in Celli Wig in Cornwall; he left neither food nor drink . . . and he also pulled Gwenhwyfar [Guinevere] out of her chair of her state, and then he struck a blow upon her."[37]

Death and Burial

Finally, there is the question of Arthur's death and burial. The Welsh tradition is that he did indeed die of wounds received

The hill of Glastonbury Tor was once an island in a swamp before being drained. Once drained, monks reportedly found two coffins containing bodies they claimed to be King Arthur and Guinevere.

at Camlannn and was buried secretly because of the effect that news of his death would have on the Britons. The Breton "Legend of St. Goeznovius," however, says only that Arthur "was summoned at last from human activity,"[38] which could mean that he withdrew from the world, possibly to become a monk.

Geoffrey writes that after the Battle of Camlannn Arthur was taken to Avalon to be healed. Geoffrey possibly knew of this tradition when he was the first to use the name, calling Avalon the Island of Apples from *aval*, the Welsh word for apple. Although —once again—numerous possible sites for Avalon are suggested, the strongest tradition associates it with Glastonbury in southeast England, only a few miles from Cadbury, one of the possible locations of the Battle of Camlannn.

The hill of Glastonbury Tor was indeed an island rising above a swamp before the area was drained. In 1191, at the time Geoffrey's history was circulating, the monks of Glastonbury Abbey reported finding a large coffin made out of a hollow oak and a lead cross with the Latin inscription "Here Lies King Arthur in the Island of Avalon." Inside were the bones of an exceptionally large and powerful man. Nearby, the monks said, was the body of a woman, presumably Guinevere.

When the monks claimed to have found Arthur's grave, pilgrims began flocking to the abbey to see it. With the pilgrims came their money. In the next century the body was buried with great ceremony before the altar in the abbey church, and pilgrimages increased.

The Glastonbury monks may well have found a body, but there is serious doubt that it was that of Arthur. The lead cross has disappeared, but drawings of it dating from the 1600s survive. The lettering is that of the 900s, not the 500s. The monks, it is suspected, may have found the body and carved the cross to bolster their claim that it was Arthur in order to raise badly needed funds for the abbey.

Summary

And so, although nothing is "known" about Arthur—no historical proof exists—putting the puzzle pieces together as best one

King Arthur's Britain

LOTHIAN
(Scotland)

River
Tweed

Merlin's
Grave

Bamburgh
Castle
(Lancelot's
Castle)

Merlin's Land

WALES

LOGRES
(England)

Carleon
Upon-Usk

Glastonbury Tor

Chalice Well Gardens

Glastonbury Abbey

Stonehenge

Tintagel Castle
(Arthur's
birthplace)

DEVON

The Round Table

CORNWALL

Camelot

St. Michael's
Mount

The Tristam
Stone

can yields a picture of a man born in far southeastern Britain in about 465, a time when the invading Anglo-Saxons were suffering defeats by the Britons, led by Ambrosius. Arthur may have been born into a royal family, but more likely was—like Ambrosius—descended from Roman or Romano-British nobility.

He was trained as a soldier and was expert in the use of swords and spears. He was a superb rider, a necessity for a cavalry commander. He rose to military prominence, probably under Ambrosius, and succeeded Ambrosius as supreme commander of the Britons about 488. He proved to be a gifted general, winning numerous battles over a wide area of Britain, leading his mounted men over the network of roads left by the Romans.

If he was a king, his headquarters was likely a fortress built atop a hill in southeastern Britain, a location from which he could lead his troops wherever needed. It would have been constructed partly out of stone but mostly of timber.

His victories culminated in a great triumph at Badon, so complete a victory over the Anglo-Saxons that the Britons enjoyed many years of relative peace afterward. Eventually, however, the Britons began to quarrel and fight among themselves. A rival named Medraut, who might have been a kinsman, mounted a challenge and was killed in a climactic battle. But the leader of the Britons was severely wounded and was carried off the battlefield, disappearing from history.

This, then, is Arthur as he was—or might have been—as a historical figure. But what of the other figures associated with Arthur—Guinevere, Lancelot, Merlin—and other aspects such as the Round Table and the Holy Grail? They belong to another realm—that of legend.

CHAPTER 4

The Layers
of Legend

I t is difficult when studying Arthur to separate fact—or what
passes for fact, given such scanty historical evidence—from
fiction. To dismiss the fiction, however, is to keep only a faint
gray outline of Arthur's story while losing the vivid splashes of
color that bring it to full flower. Ambrosius may have been a real
person, but how much more "real," in terms of our imagination,
are Merlin, Guinevere, and Lancelot? The telling of Arthur's story
over the centuries has put substance into shadow and projected
legend as reality.

This is not to say that fact and fiction are necessarily separate.
What historical figure, for instance, could so fascinate generations of readers as has Merlin the Magician? And yet Merlin, the
most fantastical character in the entire epic, is based on a historical individual.

MERLIN AND VIVIEN

Merlin the wizard was Arthur's companion and mentor from the time he was a young child, until Merlin fell in love with one of the ladies of the lake, who later locked him under a rock. Merlin warned Arthur of bad things to come, such as Guinevere's infidelity.

Merlin

Merlin appears in the *Annals of Wales* entry for the year 573: "The battle of Arfderydd between the sons of Eliffer and Gwenddolau son of Ceidio; in which battle Gwenddolau fell; Merlin went mad."[39] This Merlin was actually a bard named Myrddin Wylilt, a sort of official court poet in the service of King Gwenddolau, who lived in the northern part of Britain. He fought alongside his king in the battle and, when his master was killed, went insane and fled to the woods, where he lived as a hermit and supposedly found that he had the power to prophesy events.

Myrddin, whose name is the Welsh form of Martin, subsequently found a place in a series of twelfth-century Welsh poems in which the recluse bemoans the fate of Gwenddolau. In another somewhat later version, he is named Lailoken, but the story says that he was also called Merlynum. Although such a person probably existed, he lived too late to have been involved in Arthur's exploits.

Another version of Merlin is found in the work of Nennius. He writes that Vortigern, preparing to construct his great fortress, ordered building materials that mysteriously kept vanishing each night. He was told by his counselors that to prevent this he must find a boy born without a father, kill him, and sprinkle his blood on the site.

The Dragon Prophesy

When such a boy finally was found, he saved himself by convincing Vortigern to dig where the fortress was to be built. A pool was uncovered in which were fighting two dragons, one red and one white. The red one appeared to be on the verge of defeat, but it revived and chased the white dragon away. The boy, who said his name was Ambrose, explained that the red dragon represented the Britons—and indeed a red dragon remains the national symbol of Wales—and the white dragon the Anglo-Saxons. He said that a great leader would arise and drive the invaders away—an obvious reference to Arthur, who would appear later in his history.

Merlin later became a favorite subject of Geoffrey's. Several years before writing about Arthur, Geoffrey wrote *The Prophecies of Merlin,* in which the wizard predicts various calamities that would later befall Britain. Some scholars think Geoffrey invented the name Merlin because Myrddin sounded too much like the French word for excrement.

When Geoffrey wrote *The History of the Kings of Britain* he decided to combine Nennius's history with the Welsh legends. He got around the difference in names by simply writing that Merlin "was also called Ambrose."[40]

Merlin's Role

In Arthur's early history as described by Geoffrey and later by Malory, Merlin is a central figure. He works with Uther Pendragon to bring about Arthur's birth and later guides the young Arthur to the throne and remains at his side, sometimes advising and sometimes using his magical powers to keep the king from harm.

It seems somehow odd that a monk should relate that Arthur—a Christian king with Christian virtues whose knights (in Malory's tale) seek the Holy Grail, a strong Christian symbol—relied on someone who appears to be a pagan and a sorcerer. Possibly the story of Merlin and Arthur contains a grain of truth. Prior to Christianity the religion of the Britons was druidism, which had multiple gods and revolved around

One story involving Merlin depicts two fighting dragons, one representing the Britons, and the other representing the Anglo-Saxons. The red dragon, representing the Britons, defeats the white dragon at the end of the story.

nature worship. The Romans made every effort possible to stamp out druidism during their long occupation, but it is thought to have survived until the 600s in Ireland and in isolated pockets of Wales. The historical Arthur would not have been the first leader who, while practicing a newly dominant religion, would maintain touch with the gods of his ancestors and have a druid nearby.

Guinevere

Like Merlin, Arthur's queen Guinevere may have been based on a real person, but this is much more unlikely. Neither Nennius nor the *Annals of Wales* mentions her, and it is only in *Culhwch and Olwen*, the Welsh folk story about Arthur, that a queen first appears. The earliest manuscript for the story has been dated to about 1325, but it is believed to have originated centuries earlier.

In *Culhwch and Olwen*, the queen is named Gwenhwyvar, one of many spellings throughout the centuries that also include Guanhumara, Ginevra, and Jenefer. Gwenhwyvar can be translated from Celtic as "white ghost" or "white spirit," leading some writers to believe that the Celtic goddess Epona, sometimes represented as a white horse or white lady, might have been the original inspiration for her character.

Not much more is said about Guinevere in *Culhwch and Olwen* except that she had a sister named Gwennhwyach. The Welsh Triads reveal much more about her. Two claim that a blow given Gwenhwyvar by Gwennhwyach caused the Battle of Camlannn. Another provides an early reference to Guinevere's infidelity to Arthur, saying that in addition to three faithless wives of Britain, "one was more faithless than those three: Gwenhwyfar, Arthur's wife, since she shamed a better man than any [of the others]."[41]

The Round Table: Arthur's View

King Arthur gives Queen Guinevere his view of what the Round Table and its knights should represent in this excerpt from Alfred Lord Tennyson's *Idylls of the King,* found in *King Arthur: How History Is Invented* by Jeremy Roberts:

> A glorious company, the flower of men,
> To serve as model for the mighty world,

The original dates for both *Culhwch and Olwen* and the Welsh Triads are uncertain, and some writers have said they used Geoffrey as a basis instead of the other way around. One source that did predate Geoffrey, however, was the *Life of St. Gildas* written by a Welshman, Caradog, sometime before 1136. In Caradog's version Guinevere is kidnapped by a King Melwas and eventually rescued by Arthur, although only after he had spent a year searching for her. This abduction and rescue story seems to have set the tone for the many others involving the queen.

And be the fair beginning of a time. . . .
To break the heathen and uphold the
Christ,
To ride abroad redressing human wrongs,
To speak no slander, no, nor listen to it,
To honour his own word as if his God's,
To lead sweet lives in purest chastity . . .
Not only to keep down the base in man
But to teach high thought, and amiable
words.

Quoted in Jeremy Roberts, *King Arthur: How History Is Invented.* Minneapolis, MN: Lerner, 2001.

Combined Versions

As he did with Merlin, Geoffrey seems to have combined different versions. His Guinevere, "descended from a noble family of Romans," is abducted by Mordred while Arthur is in Europe fighting the emperor of Rome, but then she marries him "in violation of her first marriage."[42]

A few years after Geoffrey, Guinevere was developed into a major character in the story of Arthur by Chrétien. In his *Lancelot, Knight of the Cart*, written about 1180, he introduces not

only Lancelot but also the entire tragic-romantic triangle of Lancelot, Guinevere, and Arthur. Guinevere is abducted, as in Caradog—which seems to have been one of Chrétien's sources—but this time her savior is Lancelot, with whom she falls hopelessly in love. And it is this love, at first from a respectful distance, that eventually becomes adulterous, leading to the destruction of Camelot—another term coined by Chrétien.

Roundtables were highly popular among nobility, but frowned on by clergy who thought them frivolous and too costly. This is a depiction of King Arthur's Round Table.

Malory followed Chrétien and expanded the story of Guinevere and Lancelot. Brian Edward Rise, editor of an Arthurian Web site, writes that in Malory's story,

> the Queen reaches a depth that had only been hinted at by his predecessors. She becomes giving and tragically passionate. She is childless in a marriage to a man she respects but doesn't love and in love with a man she can never have. [In the end she realizes] that their [hers and Lancelot's] deeds have brought about the ruin of the noblest group the world has known.[43]

The real Guinevere, if she existed, might have had extramarital affairs, but they would not have been looked on the same way as by the medieval romantics. A Celtic queen, as she would likely have been, would have been equal in power to her husband and free to have lovers if she wished. Such a tradition would have been foreign to Chrétien and Malory, who made her an unfaithful wife as they understood fidelity in marriage.

The Round Table

It was Guinevere, at least in Malory's version, who brought to Arthur's court another major part of the story—the Round Table. The idea that Arthur surrounded himself with the most able warriors in Britain can be found in *Culhwch and Olwen*, the Welsh Triads, and Geoffrey's *History*. One document, dating from the 900s but probably based on much older oral tradition, names such figures as Sandde Angel-Face and Uchdryd Cross-Beard as being among *Some of King Arthur's Wonderful Men*.

The Round Table itself, however, was first mentioned by a monk named Wace who in about 1155 wrote *Roman de Brut*, based on Geoffrey, in which he related that since each of Arthur's knights

> pained himself to be the hardiest champion, and none would count him the least praiseworthy, Arthur made the Round Table, so reputed of the Britons. This Round Table was ordained of Arthur that when his fair fellowship sat to meat their chairs should be high alike, their service equal, and none before or after his comrade.[44]

The round shape was a departure from the normal long, rectangular table, at the head of which sat the king, with others seated according to rank, the highest being closest to the king.

This woodcut shows the knights seated at King Arthur's Round Table. The most well known knights were Lancelot, Galahad, Gawain, Tristram, Mordred, Perceval, Bedivere, and Kay.

Layamon's Story

There are other versions of how the Round Table came about. The *Brut,* written by an Englishman named Layamon in about 1215, says an all-out brawl erupted in Arthur's court over who was to sit where. Shortly afterward Arthur happened to meet a carpenter who had heard of the problem and offered to build a round table "exceeding fair, that thereat may sit sixteen hundred and more, all turn about, so that none be without; without and within, man against man."[45] Frenchman Robert de Boron, writing at about the same time, has Merlin creating the table as an imitation of the 13-seat Grail Table supposedly constructed by Joseph of Arimathea to commemorate the Last Supper.

The seating capacity of the Round Table varies wildly, from 13 in the French *Didot-Perceval* all the way to Layamon's 1,600, including Malory's 150 and many more. The number, if such a table ever existed, probably would not have been much more than 50, since such a table would be 50 feet in diameter. Anything larger would have made a group discussion difficult if not impossible.

The Winchester Table

Actually, a centuries-old round table does exist in the English city of Winchester, where Malory placed Camelot. Scientific examination, however, has dated its construction at about 1275, and so it could have been part of a roundtable held by King Edward I. These events, seeking to reproduce what people believed Arthur's court to have been like, featured days of jousting (mock combat), feasting, and dancing. Roundtables were highly popular among the nobility, but frowned on by clergy who thought them frivolous and too costly.

One such roundtable in 1344 inspired King Edward III of England to create a band of knights similar to Arthur's, but instead of calling it the Round Table, it was known as the Order of the Garter. It was neither the first nor the last such imitation of Arthur's fellowship. The Order of St. George had been founded by the king of Hungary in 1325, and the French Order of the Star would come in 1351, followed by many others.

Such organizations, however, bore little resemblance to what Arthur's band of Celtic warriors would have been. As Rodney Castleden writes in *King Arthur: The Truth Behind the Legend*, "The later and highly elaborated, highly romanticized tales of the Round Table knights must really be set aside in reconstructing the historical Arthur, but it is nevertheless likely that they represent a genuine, if highly coloured, tradition based on a sixth century reality."[46]

"QUOTE"

"[In the end Guinevere realizes] that their [hers and Lancelot's] deeds have brought about the ruin of the noblest group the world has known."

— Editor of Arthurian Web site describing the events leading to the downfall of Camelot.

The Knights

If the Round Table is a fable, however, it is possible that some of the knights who were said to have sat there were real. The round table on display in Winchester, which was repainted by order of King Henry VIII in 1522, carries 25 names. The best known are Lancelot, Galahad, Gawain, Tristram, Mordred, Perceval, Bedivere, and Kay. Of these knights, the most popular in literature by far has been Lancelot, but his origin is the most obscure.

He first appears in minor roles in Chrétien's early poems and then becomes the star-crossed lover of Guinevere in *Le Chevalier de la Charette*, or *Knight of the Cart*. His role is expanded in a German work, *Lanzelet*, and he dominates a series of later French prose works known as the Vulgate Cycle.

How Lancelot came to be connected with Arthur is unknown. There is no Celtic equivalent for the name, and he does not figure in any English version until Malory. The best guess is that Lancelot was the hero of several obscure French folk tales and was incorporated by Chrétien into Arthur's story.

Tristram

Tristram, on the other hand, appears to have roots in Britain, though just where is not clear. His name is a derivation of the Pictish name Drust, and his kingdom of Lyonesse may be Leonais, an old French name for an area of what is now Scotland. This would seem to mean that he came from the north of Britain, but it would not explain how he became connected with King Mark of Cornwall, far to the south. If Tristram were Mark's nephew, as in many versions, it would be possible, but he may have been Mark's son. In 1962 a 6th-century gravestone was discovered in Cornwall that bore the inscription "Drustanus, son of Cunomorus," the latter being another name for Mark.

Tristram appears as Drystan in *Culhwch and Olwen* and in other Welsh tales, but the earliest story of his tragic love affair with Isolde, King Mark's wife, comes in the works of two French poets in the 1100s. The tale itself, however, may be much older, and some experts believe that Chrétien and others may have based their Lancelot-Guinevere stories on Tristram and Isolde. Both have endured among the greatest love stories of all time, rendered in operas, musicals, motion pictures, and works of art.

Other prominent members of the Round Table, unlike Lancelot and Tristram, have a much firmer Welsh pedigree. Kay, who in Geoffrey's version is Arthur's foster brother, is a prominent character in *Culhwch and Olwen*, where his name is Cai Hir, or Kay the Tall. Gawain is based on the Welsh hero Gwalchmei, who in *Culhwch and Olwen* is Arthur's nephew, just as in Geoffrey. Bedivere and Perceval—later versions of Bedwyr and Peredur, respectively—also come from Welsh folk tales.

Galahad

Galahad, however, seems to be a much later invention than any of the others. He is first mentioned in the French Post-Vulgate Cycle written about 1235 in connection with the search for the Holy

Galahad, seen looking into Arthur's tomb, was portrayed as the perfect knight, and the only one of Arthur's knights pure enough to find the Holy Grail.

Roundtables were
highly popular
among the nobility,
but frowned on by
clergy who thought
them frivolous and
too costly.

Grail. He is the illegitimate son of Lancelot and Elaine, daughter of King Pelles, the keeper of the Grail. The romances portray him as the perfect knight—valorous and chaste—the only one of Arthur's knights pure enough to find the Grail. Some writers think Galahad was intended to be a reincarnation of Jesus, and his name may come from the biblical area known as Gilead.

While many of Arthur's knights have their roots in Celtic literature, so perhaps does their most famous exploit—the quest for the Holy Grail. This highly evocative Christian symbol is thought by some scholars to have begun as a magic cauldron in pre-Christian Welsh folklore. Such objects were supposed to have such powers as healing wounds or illnesses, raising the dead, or providing never-ending supplies of food and wine.

One such tale, the *Spoils of Annwfn* attributed to the bard Taliesin, involves Arthur. In it Arthur and his companions visit Annwfn, the ancient Welsh version of heaven, intending to steal a magic cauldron. Of three shiploads of knights, only eight, including Arthur, survive, and his mission is not accomplished. A very similar story appears in *Culhwch and Olwen*.

Origin of the Grail

Other experts disagree with the notion of a Celtic origin for the Grail and claim that it began as a purely Christian symbol in France, possibly through the influence of the Cistercians. This order of monks, founded in 1098, tended toward mysticism and sought to bring more spirituality to the rite of Communion. In their ritual, the cup, which received scant mention and little glorification in the Bible, became a much more profound symbol.

Thus with the blessing of the church, which generally disapproved of folk tales with pagan overtones, the Holy Grail became a popular topic of fiction. Chrétien penned the first account sometime about 1180. Perceval, not Arthur, was the hero of the story, and the *graal*, a French adaptation of the Latin word for "dish," does not have as much significance as the Communion wafer on it.

About 10 years later Robert de Boron gave the Grail a much deeper meaning. He writes that Joseph of Arimathea used the cup from the Last Supper to catch drops of Jesus's blood at his Crucifixion. Later, the significance and powers of the cup having been explained to him by the risen Jesus, Joseph and some followers take the Grail to Britain.

Several versions of a quest for the Holy Grail followed. Most featured Perceval, and one had Gawain finding the holy cup. The Vulgate Cycle introduced first Lancelot then Lancelot's son Galahad into the story, and it was the Galahad version that was picked up and made famous by Malory and later in Alfred Lord Tennyson's epic poem *Idylls of the King*. Thus, even though perhaps rooted in Celtic legend, the Holy Grail would seem to be a fictional creation and have no connection to a historical Arthur.

Who, however, was the historical Arthur? If such a person indeed existed and achieved such fame and glory, why has no firm evidence of that existence—no letters, monuments, or other records—been found? Was Arthur, as some have suggested, a nickname and, if so, for what historical figure? The list of candidates is long. All have their patrons, but no one has come up with any proof.

CHAPTER 5

The "Real" King Arthur

History, like nature, tends to resist a vacuum. Just as air will rush in to fill empty spaces, so too will suppositions, conjectures, theories, and speculations flood into the gaps left by an absence of facts. Thus, since specific details about King Arthur are few and far between, scholars over the centuries have not been shy about putting forth their own ideas as to who he might have been, if he existed at all.

Indeed, one of the most long-standing notions has been that Arthur is mostly, if not entirely, a product of fiction and should not be considered in any historical context. In his *History of English Affairs,* written about 1198, the monk William of Newburgh accused Geoffrey of "inventing the most ridiculous fictions" and trying to "dignify them with the name of authentic history."[47]

Much later, in 1848, Thomas Babington Macaulay wrote in his *History of England*, "It is only in Britain that an age of fable

[Arthur] completely separates two ages of truth. . . . Arthur and Mordred are mythical persons, whose very existence may be questioned, and whose adventures must be classed with those of Hercules and Romulus."[48] More recently, historian J.N.L. Myres wrote, "No figure on the borderline of history and mythology has wasted more of the historian's time."[49]

Other critics have been less harsh. Perhaps the most telling argument against Arthur's existence was that Gildas, who lived during what would have been Arthur's lifetime and career, never mentions him by name. This silence, Sir Frank Stenton wrote in 1943, "may suggest that the Arthur of history was a less imposing figure than the Arthur of legend, but it should not be allowed to remove him from the sphere of history."[50]

Lucius Artorius Castus

Some experts, logically enough, have concentrated their search for the "real" Arthur among the few documented figures in ancient Britain who bore that name. The first candidate, whose cause was first promoted in the 1920s and later taken up by historian P.F.J. Turner in 1993, was Lucius Artorius Castus.

Castus, a member of the well-to-do Artorii family of southern Italy, was born about 150 and entered the army. He was promoted rapidly, eventually becoming a *praefectus*, or commander, of the Sixth Legion, which was based in Britain and won numerous victories over the Picts. Having remained loyal during a mutiny, he was rewarded with the title of *dux*, a general commanding two or more legions, and shortly after 185 led a successful expedition to Brittany.

There is no way, of course, that this Arthur could be the same general who defeated the Anglo-Saxons at the Battle of Badon some 300 years later, but there are interesting parallels between Castus's career and the various accounts of Arthur. The legion he commanded in Britain was charged with guarding Hadrian's Wall. The battles his legion fought were in the same area as some of those listed by Nennius among Arthur's victories. Specifically, one of his major campaigns was against the Caledonii tribe, and one of the battles in Nennius's list is the Caledonian Wood.

The most striking parallel, however, is that both Castus and Arthur—at least Geoffrey's Arthur—win a major battle in northern Britain, regroup their forces in the city of York, and then embark on a military expedition in present-day France. While Arthur is said to have fought Roman legions, it is possible that Castus did the same, putting down a rebellion led by an ex-soldier.

While there is nothing else in Castus's biography that would indicate a connection with Arthur, the parallels are enough for Turner to call him "the real king Arthur."[51] And Arthurian scholar Linda A. Malcor writes that "the parallels between Castus and Arthur are striking not only in their number but also in the variety of levels on which they occur. Castus meets all of the qualifications required for him to be the historical catalyst for the legends."[52]

Arthur of Dalriada

If Castus came too early to have been Nennius's hero, Arthur of Dalriada came too late. Born sometime about 575, he was one of the sons of King Aedan of Delriada, who ruled an area that encompassed southwestern Scotland and northwestern Ireland.

At this time Dalriada, which had been founded by immigrants from Ireland in about 500, were allied with the British against the Picts. A biography of Saint Columba written in about 700 tells that Aedan had four sons—Artuir, Echoid Find, Domingart, and a younger son, Echoid Buide, who the saint prophesied would succeed to the throne. The story goes on:

> All these things were completely fulfilled afterwards, in their time. For Artuir and Echoid Find were slain a little while later, in the battle of the Miathi [a Pictish tribe]. . . . Domingart was killed in a rout of the battle in England [presumably against the advancing Anglo-Saxons]. And Echoid Buide succeeded to the throne after his father.[53]

This is the only clear reference to Arthur of Dalriada, but it is important because the bard Aneurin wrote in *Y Gododdin* a century earlier and in the same locale that while a hero of the Votadini was a powerful warrior, he was no Arthur. The Votadini, although Pictish, were—like Dalriada—allied with the British, and Aneurin may have been referring to the slain prince.

Historian Richard Barber, Arthur of Dalriada's chief proponent, suggests this is the case, adding that Arthur, named first among Aedan's sons, may have been the eldest and a hero of many victories. "He therefore meets the criterion of a local, contemporary hero of the type celebrated elsewhere in that poem,"[54] Barber writes. The fact that Aneurin does not further identify this Arthur also would seem to indicate that those who heard of or read the poem would be familiar with the person.

A Northern Arthur

Author Norma Lorre Goodrich also proposes an Arthur based in the north of Britain. In her book *King Arthur* she suggests that Arthur was a descendant, on his mother's side, of Cunedda, king of the Votadini—a Pictish tribe in the north who later may have migrated to the kingdom of Gwynedd in north Wales. She generally agrees with Geoffrey that Arthur came from Roman nobility on his father's side and possibly was a direct descendant of Emperor Constantine.

She places his birth at Caelverlock Castle near Dumfries on the western shore of northern Britain near the present-day border between England and Scotland. "The original name of that castle and sandy shore," she writes, "may have been something like 'Tintagel,' but in a British and not a Cornish form, like 'Dun Dagel.'"[55]

Her reasoning for this location is that Arthur's father likely commanded troops at a nearby camp and that there was an abbey close at hand where he would have been educated. In addition, a small lake to the west is known by local historians as "Arthur's Lake."

Arthur's Capital

Arthur's capital, she writes, was nearby at the city of Carlisle, and she seeks to show that almost all the 12 battles recorded by Nennius were fought in the north. She places Badon not near Bath, as do most scholars, but near the large hill at Dumbarton near present-day Glasgow.

Since Arthur's capital was at Carlisle, she writes, it was likely near there that Camlannn, the final battle, was fought. She identifies Camboglanna, the westernmost fort on Hadrian's Wall, just a short distance from Carlisle, as the probable site. From there, she says, Arthur was taken via ship through the Solway Firth across the Irish Sea to the Isle of Man, which she identifies as Avalon.

Goodrich presents an intriguing theory, but it is not one that persuades fellow researcher Castleden. He writes in *King Arthur: The Truth Behind the Legend* that Goodrich depends too much on very tenuous links with such locales as Caelverlock. "Ultimately," he writes, "there is too much bending of cultural realities both contemporary and ancient for her case to convince."[56]

Southern Arthurs

At least two southern Arthurs can be added to the northern Arthur of Dalriada. One, whose name appears both as Arthwyr and Arthrwys, was the son of King Meurig of Gwent, a small kingdom in southeastern Wales. He lived in the mid-600s, perhaps ruling jointly with his father, and died about 655. This is too late for him to have figured in Nennius's battles, but scholars who point to him as the real Arthur have various explanations. Some claim that the confusion arises because his exploits are mixed up with those of a warrior named Arthwys, who lived and fought in the north a century earlier. Others say Arthwyr/Arthrwys lived a century earlier than is generally thought and that his father, although his real name was Meurig, was known as Uther Pendragon, or "wonderful commander" in Welsh.

Yet another Arthur is known to have ruled the Welsh kingdom

of Dyfed, a large area in southwestern Wales. Like Dalriada, Dyfed was settled by Irish immigrants, probably in the late 300s. No dates are given for his reign, but studies of separate Irish and Welsh genealogies estimate his birth at somewhere between 580 and 620—again too late for Nennius's battles.

Other historians have not tried to discover various Arthurs who fit the mold provided by Nennius and Geoffrey. Instead, they looked for historical figures who were not named Arthur, but who might have earned the nickname from the Welsh word for bear because of their military might or because they fit the time and place.

Owain Ddantgwyn

Phillips and Keatman identify just such a person in their book *King Arthur: The True Story*. Their candidate is Owain Ddantgwyn, named in genealogies as ruler of the combined Welsh kingdoms of Powys and Gwynedd. Nothing is known of Owain but his name. He is not recorded as having been a great warrior or ruler, but Phillips and Keatmen present a cohesive case for considering him.

First of all, he ruled at the right time—at least if the date of 493 is accepted for the Battle of Badon, which Gildas writes was fought 44 years after the landing of the Anglo-Saxons, thought to have occurred in 449. Owain's father, Enniaun Girt, became king in 480, and Owain's nephew and successor, Cunneglasus, began his rule in 520. This would make Owain either prince or king at the time of the Battle of Badon.

Second, he ruled in the right place—provided a series of assumptions by the authors are correct. Gwynedd, they write, was the most powerful British kingdom in the late 400s, a time when others to the east had been overrun by the Anglo-Saxons. Thus, it would have been logical that it was Arthur's base of power.

Furthermore, Nennius writes that Ambrosius was closely associated with Gwynedd earlier in the 400s, and a hill fort bearing the Welsh version of his name, Emrys, is found there. Since Arthur is generally thought to have fought alongside Ambrosius, this, too, would place Arthur in Gwynedd.

The Dragon Symbol

One other piece of evidence connects Arthur with Gwynedd. Sometime in the mid-400s, the kings of Gwynedd adopted the red dragon as their symbol—the same red dragon that remains the national symbol of Wales. Some ancient Welsh poems refer to these kings as the "head dragons" or pendragon, and Geoffrey named Uther Pendragon as Arthur's father.

Arthur, however, could not have been a direct descendant of Ambrosius, at least not if, as the *Annals of Wales* relates, the kings of Gwynedd were descended from Cunneda, a warrior whose roots are far to the north in present-day Scotland. This is where the Votadini enter the picture.

The Votadini were the Pictish tribe whose bard Aneurin wrote *Y Gododdin*. They had been allies of the Romans against the wilder tribes to the north and after the departure of the legions maintained friendly relations with the Britons. In the 400s, however, they were under attack from the north (the Picts), the south (the Anglo-Saxons), and the west (the Scotii invaders from Ireland). Phillips and Keatman surmise that a large body of Votadini, led by Cunneda, were persuaded by Ambrosius to immigrate to Gwynedd, perhaps to help him overthrow Vortigern, whose base likewise might have been in the same area.

Archaeological evidence has supported such a movement of the Votadini to north Wales. Distinctive pottery similar to that found in the Votadini homeland in Scotland has also been unearthed in Gwynedd and furthermore has been dated to the late 500s.

The Votadini Connection

The connection of the Votadini to Gwynedd is significant for two reasons. First, if Arthur were indeed one of a line of kings descended from the Pictish tribe, it would explain why Nennius wrote that he fought "with" all the kings of Britain, implying that Arthur himself was not British.

Second, it would also help explain Aneurin's reference in *Y Gododdin* that an otherwise valiant Votadini warrior was "no Arthur." If, as many scholars believe, Arthur's roots were in southwestern Britain—either Wales or Cornwall—it is hard to understand why a poet far to the north should invoke his name a century later. But the question is answered if Aneurin was referring to a hero descended from the Votadini.

Phillips and Keatman go on to speculate that Owain-Arthur, although having originated in and ultimately become king of both Gwynedd and Powys, first established his power base in Powys. Their evidence is a passage from Gildas in which the monk fumes at a king named Cunneglasus, calling him "you bear, ride of many and driver of the chariot of the bear's household."[57] Who was the bear—*arth* in Welsh—and where was his household?

It was not Gwynedd, which at the time Gildas was writing was ruled by a king named Maglocunnus, but more likely was Powys, which was adjacent to Gwynedd. This reference to what may have been a nickname would make Owain Ddantgwyn king of Powys and perhaps Cunneglasus's father.

Viroconium

The case for Powys is strengthened further by archaeological studies of the old Roman city of Viroconium located there. Archaeology has shown that in the years after 450—about the time of Vortigern—Viroconium was the largest, most important city held by the Britons, since London, York, and Lincoln were subject to attack by Anglo-Saxons or Picts. Thus, it would have been logical for Vortigern and then both Ambrosius and Arthur to locate their capital there. Indeed, ancient tombstones have shown that Viroconium was inhabited by the Votadini.

Another possible link between Viroconium and Arthur is that archaeologists have found that the city was largely abandoned about 520. Could this have been a few years after the Battle of Camlannn at which Arthur fought Mordred and was wounded, perhaps fatally? The *Annals of Wales* puts the date of Camlannn at 537, but it also dates the Battle of Badon at 516. If, however, the date of 493 for Badon is correct, then Camlannn would have been in about 514.

The authors go on to suggest that if Owain Ddantgwyn fought a decisive battle shortly before 520, it might have been against a confederation of British rebels and their Saxon allies. The Saxons would have been led by Cerdic, founder of what would become the kingdom of Wessex, and the British by Cunomorous, king of Dumnonia, an area encompassing Cornwall in far southeastern Britain. The "Cun" part of Cunomorous's name indicates that he was a descendant of Cunneda. Thus, it is possible that Cunomorous was Owain's nephew just as Modred was Arthur's

Churchill
on Arthur

The popularity of Geoffrey of Monmouth's account of King Arthur in *History of the Kings of Britain* was of the utmost influence in establishing Arthur as a historical figure. Subsequent writers, including such eminent historians as David Hume and Thomas Babington Macaulay, accepted him as fact even though they rejected various fictitious aspects. So did Winston Churchill, whose description in *A History of the English-Speaking Peoples* clearly had reference to the recently fought war against Nazi Germany:

> They [historians] are ready to believe however that there was a great British warrior, who kept the light of civilization burning against all the storms that beat, and that behind his sword

there sheltered a faithful following of which the memory did not fail. . . . And wherever men are fighting against barbarism, tyranny, and massacre, for freedom, law, and honour, let them remember that the fame of their deeds, even though they themselves be exterminated, may perhaps be celebrated as long as the world rolls round. Let us then declare that King Arthur and his noble knights, guarding the Sacred Flame of Christianity and the theme of a world order, sustained by valour, physical strength, and good horses and armour, slaughtered innumerable hosts of foul barbarians and set decent folk an example for all time.

Winston Churchill, *A History of the English-Speaking Peoples.* New York: Dodd, Mead, 1956.

nephew—as well as his son—in Geoffrey's story.

The claim that Owain Ddantgwyn was Arthur is logical and precise, but it is a tapestry woven with threads of speculation. Remove a single thread and the entire fabric might fall apart. Castleden does just that in his book *King Arthur: The Truth Behind the Legend*. He writes that there is insufficient evidence that Gwynedd was the most powerful kingdom in Britain in the late 400s, that other cities such as Carlisle or Cadbury could have been the capital of Ambrosius and Arthur rather than Viroconium, and that other kingdoms besides Gwynedd used the dragon as a symbol.

Riotimus

Another candidate put forward as the "real" Arthur is Riotimus, the so-called king of the Britons who led an expeditionary force to Gaul. This is the view of Ashe, who in his book *The Discovery of King Arthur* weaves yet another fabric that, while not as complex as that of Phillips and Keatman, yields as interesting a picture.

The mistake made by most searchers after Arthur, Ashe writes, is to depend exclusively on older Welsh sources such as Gildas, Nennius, and the various poems. These, he writes, fail to provide a "clear-cut, trustworthy statement" on which to build a case. He suggests going beyond "layers of legend" in search of facts.[58]

Ashe discovers these facts to have been written centuries later by Geoffrey, so often dismissed as having invented most of his account of Arthur. He concentrates on the large portion of Geoffrey's story—Arthur's expeditions to Gaul to battle the Roman Emperor Lucius—that is found nowhere in Welsh sources and is often discounted as pure fiction.

Were there, however, actual events on which Geoffrey's account could have been based? Yes, argues Ashe, and he cites the career of Riotimus, who was the only British ruler known to have led an army into Gaul. In addition, like Geoffrey's Arthur, Riotimus suffered a betrayal and disappeared from history after a climactic battle.

Riotimus's expedition into Gaul can be accurately dated using Geoffrey's references. For instance, Geoffrey writes that Arthur was the grandson of a king named Constantine, and Constantine is known to have died before 429, when Vortigern was ruling. The career of a grandson of Constantine, therefore, would have been very unlikely to extend into the 500s.

Furthermore, in describing Arthur's exploits, Geoffrey refers to the Roman emperor Leo, who ruled from 457 to 474. He also mentions a Pope Sulpicius, which may represent a misspelling of Simplicius, pope from 468 to 483. This fixes Arthur's campaign in Gaul between 468 and 474.

Ashe acknowledges some difficulties in identifying Riotimus as Geoffrey's Arthur. Why, for instance, did Geoffrey use the name Arthur instead of Riotimus? A possible explanation is that his name was, indeed, Artorius, but that sources in Gaul referred to him as Riotimus because that name could be translated as "high king" and thus was a title rather than the person's name.

And then the question arises about who the enemy was. Arthur fought the Romans, but Riotomus fought with the Romans against the Visigoths. Ashe explains that Geoffrey, in making Arthur an epic hero, had to provide a suitably formidable foe and thus, for "literary purpose,"[59] made the change.

Mordred, who developed a bitter hatred for Arthur, delivered the blow from which Arthur would later die. During the same battle Arthur delivered the blow that would result in Mordred's death.

Another problem is that Geoffrey gives 542 as the year Arthur was taken to Avalon to cure his wounds. Such a date would be completely out of sequence not only with Riotimus but with other dates proposed for the Battle of Camlannn between Arthur and Mordred, except possibly for the 537 date in the *Annals of Wales*. Ashe's explanation is that a 28-year difference in ancient methods of dating may have given a date of 442 for what actually happened in 470, and that Geoffrey, seeking to make things fit with a later date for Badon, simply added 100 years.

The Later Battles

The more troublesome question in dating events, however, is one of how to connect a Riotimus-Arthur, whose final battle somewhere in Gaul was in about 470, with the battles of Badon and Camlannn, generally thought to have occurred much later. How could he have been there? Ashe suggests that he was not.

One explanation is that "the Arthur of legend and romance combines two originals. The first would be Arthur-Riothamus, the second a warrior who led the Britons at Badon and fell at Camlannn."[60] Ashe's second suggestion is that Arthur's name was somehow projected onto his followers who returned from Gaul and—decades later—defeated the Saxons at Badon. He raises the possibility that poems contained "praise for the deed's of 'Arthur's men,' and this became 'Arthur and his men,' turning an honorary presence into a literal one, which there was ample willingness to believe."[61]

In summary, Ashe states that the historical Arthur so many scholars have sought was "a construct made of Welsh odds and ends, based on the impression that a real person lurked behind them."[62] That person, he concludes, is Riotimus.

Other Views

There are other—many other—theories about who King Arthur might have been. Sharon Turner proposed in 1805 that Arthur might have been the son of Mouric, king of Glamorganshire in Scotland. Trelawney Dayrell Reed dismissed the historical Arthur as the bastard son of Ambrosius's brother, sent north by his uncle to fight the Picts.

Baram Blackett and Alan Wilson identified Arthur with King Meurig of Gwent but proposed that they might have been one and the same instead of son and father. And Sir John Rhys suggested that the historic Arthur, whoever he might have been, has been grafted onto an ancient British god whose name was somehow similar and that, rather than treating him as a cultural hero, "he should in fact rather be treated, let us say, as a Celtic Zeus."[63]

Indeed, there seem to be almost as many Arthurs as there are Arthurian historians. This is hardly surprising given the lack of hard facts. Instead, historians must rely on a handful of clues that are tantalizingly vague. Seen dimly across the centuries they seem, like a signpost glimpsed through a thick fog, to point in almost any direction.

EPILOGUE

Who . . .
or What?

O f all the various answers to the question of who Arthur might have been, are any correct? Perhaps none of them, and on the other hand perhaps all of them, are true. One theory may not be as good as any other—as well-founded in dusty genealogies or supported by archaeology—but none can be dismissed. Only some new discovery—a document or inscription brought to light—can blow away the fog and reveal the true, historical Arthur.

The difficulty of pinpointing who Arthur was, however, has made it easier for people throughout history to construct what he was. He is almost a blank canvas on which can be painted whatever picture is desired, mixing colors from a palette made up of folktales, poems, and bits and pieces of history, much of which might not be accurate.

Merlin had a marble block placed in the courtyard of a great church in London. The block held an iron anvil into which was stuck a sword. Many tried to pull the sword out of the stone but all failed until the young Arthur succeeded.

IVRE REX BRITANNIÆ

HOW ARTHVR DREW THE SWORD

What the various pictures may look like will depend on the artists and what they want to portray. As Nicholas Higham writes in *King Arthur: Myth-Making and History*,

What becomes most apparent from an overview of the entire period discussed, from the fifth and sixth centuries right through to the end of the twentieth, is the sense in which Arthur's historicity has depended primarily on the contemporary political and cultural positioning of particular authors and their audiences, leaving his role in historical narratives at all periods subject to the ever-changing purposes of historians and the predilections of their audiences. . . . Rather, in all cases, then as now, the past was pressed into the service of the present and was subject to the immediate, and highly variable, purposes of political theology.[64]

The Christian King

Arthur can become, for instance, a Christian king fighting for his religion against pagan invaders. Such a view was popular during the Crusades, and some knightly orders, such as the Templars, were created in an imitation of the Round Table.

He can be viewed as the valiant warrior, who rallies his strife-torn people and beats back the invading barbarians. The people of Britain might have pictured Winston Churchill in such a role during the darkest days of World War II when an invasion from Nazi Germany seemed not only possible, but inevitable.

Arthur can be a paragon of virtue, an embodiment of the code of chivalry that promises to protect the weak and poor, to right wrongs, to come to the aid of all that seek it. Such was the idea behind the Order of the Garter founded by King Edward in 1344.

He can be seen, particularly by the Welsh, as a cultural hero whose leadership kept the Anglo-Saxons from completely overrunning Britain, thus providing breathing space in which that culture might find a way to survive. Ashe considers him a political hero, as well, writing that not only culture but also aspects of government developed during this half-century of breathing space, and that the delay might have altered British history by delaying and modifying the kind of absolute monarchy that emerged in France.

The *Restitutor*

Perhaps Arthur's more enduring role, however, has been that of a *restitutor*, or restorer, one who can bring back a golden age whether it be one of peace, prosperity, military might, national pride, cultural prominence, or all at once. Such an aspect, however, requires that he be immortal, and this has been made possible by the legends. Arthur did not die, writes the author of the "Life of St. Goeznovius," but instead "was summoned at last from human activity."[65] His body was not buried at Glastonbury, but rather he still dwells on the magic Isle of Avalon or sleeps in a cave, ready to be called forth by his people in time of need. As Castleden writes, "Arthur himself was seen by the British, even after his abdication and disappearance, as the ultimate Rescuer, the prototype and still the stereotype of the knight in shining armor."[66]

And who is to say that that knight has not ridden to the rescue, at least in a figurative sense? Not only did the British overcome heavy odds against the Nazis in the twentieth century but also in the thirteenth against the French in the Hundred Years' War, in the fifteenth with the defeat of the mighty Spanish Armada, and in the nineteenth when they stood virtually alone against Napoléon Bonaparte.

This is not to say that Arthur and his spirit are the exclusive property of the British. The story of Arthur, Guinevere, the Round Table, and its knights have known no boundaries. Ashe writes,

> Here is a spellbinding theme, national, yet transcending nationality. . . . The Undying King is a strangely powerful reminder that there is Something Else. By nurturing that awareness, and a questing spirit, his fame may have its effect on human thinking. It may influence history again, outside movements and governments; and not only in Britain.[67]

Scholars and archaeologists will no doubt continue their own quest—that for the "real" King Arthur—digging through ancient manuscripts and into grass-covered hills. Perhaps, however, it would be best if that final piece of the puzzle remains undiscovered lest reality corrupt the legend. It can be argued that instead of a historical figure, the world needs an ideal—something to hold in mind as a vision of what could be. So the scholars and archaeologists, as they search, would do well to recall the words of the poet William Butler Yeats: "Tread softly because you tread on my dreams."[68]

NOTES

Chapter 1: The Britain of Legend

1. Sir Thomas Malory, *Le Morte d'Arthur: Book 1*, chap. 5, *Arthurian Legend.* www.arthurian-legend.com.
2. Malory, *Le Morte d'Arthur: Book 3*, chap. 15.
3. Malory, *Le Morte d'Arthur: Book 4*, chap. 2.
4. Malory, *Le Morte d'Arthur: Book 8*, chap. 5.
5. Malory, *Le Morte d'Arthur: Book 6*, chap. 1.
6. Malory, *Le Morte d'Arthur: Book 12*, chap. 14.
7. Malory, *Le Morte d'Arthur: Book 17*, chap. 22.
8. Malory, *Le Morte d'Arthur: Book 21*, chap. 7.

Chapter 2: The Britain of History

9. Gildas, *Concerning the Ruin of Britain,* Medieval Sourcebook, Fordham University. www.fordham.edu.
10. Bede, *The Ecclesiastical History of the English Nation*, Christian Classics Ethereal Library. www.ccel.org.
11. Bede, *The Ecclesiastical History of the English Nation.*
12. Gildas, *Concerning the Ruin of Britain.*
13. *The Anglo-Saxon Chronicles*, trans. Anne Savage. New York: Crescent, 1995, p. 29.
14. Gildas, *Concerning the Ruin of Britain.*
15. Gildas, *Concerning the Ruin of Britain.*
16. Gildas, *Concerning the Ruin of Britain.*
17. Quoted in Geoffrey Ashe, *The Discovery of King Arthur.* New York: Henry Holt, 1985, p. 53.
18. Gildas, *Concerning the Ruin of Britain.*

Chapter 3: The Historical Arthur

19. Nennius, *Historia Brittonum,* Medieval Sourcebook, Fordham University. www.fordham.edu.
20. Nennius, *Historia Brittonum.*

21. Quoted in Graham Phillips and Martin Keatman, *King Arthur: The True Story.* London: Century Random House, 1992, p. 125.
22. Quoted in Rodney Castleden, *King Arthur: The Truth Behind the Legend.* London: Routledge, 2000, p. 28.
23. Quoted in Jack Lindsay, *Arthur and His Times: Britain in the Dark Ages.* New York: Barnes and Noble, 1966, p. 220.
24. Nennius, *Historia Brittonum.*
25. Nennius, *Historia Brittonum.*
26. Quoted in Richard Barber, *The Figure of Arthur.* Totowa, NJ: Rowman and Littlefield, 1972, p. 96.
27. Quoted in Michael O'Neal, ed., *King Arthur: Opposing Viewpoints.* San Diego: Greenhaven, 1992, p. 39.
28. Lindsay, *Arthur and His Times*, p. 216.
29. William, Chaplain to Bishop Eudo of Leon, "The Legend of St. Goeznovius," *Britannia: Sources to British History.* www.britannia.com.
30. Quoted in Sheila Brynjulfson, "Geoffrey of Monmouth and the History of the Kings of Britain," *Vortigern Studies.* www.vortigernstudies.org.uk /artgue/guestsheila3.htm.
31. John Leland, *The Itinerary of John Leland, Antiquary*, University of Rochester Camelot Project. www.lib.rochester.edu.
32. Nennius, *Historia Brittonum.*
33. Gildas, *Concerning the Ruin of Britain.*
34. Gildas, *Concerning the Ruin of Britain.*
35. *Annals of Wales (Annales Cambriae)*, Medieval Sourcebook, Fordham University. www.fordham.edu.
36. *Annals of Wales (Annales Cambriae).*

37. The Quest: An Arthurian Resource, "Sir Mordred the Traitor." www.uidaho.edu/student_orgs.

38. William, Chaplain to Bishop Eudo of Leon, "The Legend of St. Goeznovius."

Chapter 4: The Layers of Legend

39. *Annals of Wales (Annales Cambriae)*.

40. Geoffrey of Monmouth, *History of the Kings of Britain*, trans. Aaron Thompson. Cambridge, ONT: In Parentheses, 1999. www.yorku.ca.

41. Quoted in University of British Columbia Faculty of Arts, "Guenevere." http://faculty.arts.ubc.ca.

42. Geoffrey of Monmouth, *Arthurian Passages from The History of the Kings of Britain*, ed. and trans. J.A. Giles, Camelot Project, University of Rochester. www.lib.rochester.edu.

43. Brian Edward Rise, "Guinevere," *Encyclopedia Mythica*. www.pantheon.org.

44. Wace, *The "Arthurian" Portions of the Roman de Brut*, trans. Eugene Mason. Cambridge, ON: In Parentheses, 1999. www.yorku.ca.

45. Layamon, *Brut*, trans. Eugene Mason, Project Gutenberg. www.gutenberg.org.

46. Castleden, *King Arthur,* p. 45.

Chapter 5: The "Real" King Arthur

47. William of Newburgh, *The History of William of Newburgh*, Medieval Sourcebook, Fordham University. www.fordham.edu.

48. Quoted in Britannia, "King Arthur: Commentary—What the Historians and Writers Say About Him." www.britannia.com.

49. Quoted in Britannia, "King Arthur: Commentary."

50. Quoted in Britannia, "King Arthur: Commentary."

51. Quoted in Britannia, "King Arthur: Commentary."

52. Linda A. Malcor, "Lucius Artorius Castus: Part 2." *Heroic Age*, no. 2, Autumn/Winter 1999.www.mun.ca.

53. Quoted in Barber, *The Figure of Arthur*, p. 29.

54. Barber, *The Figure of Arthur*, p. 31.

55. Norma Lorre Goodrich, *King Arthur*. New York: Harper and Row, 1986, p. 15.

56. Castleden, *King Arthur*, p. 124.

57. Gildas, *Concerning the Ruin of Britain*.

58. Ashe, *The Discovery of King Arthur*, p. 87.

59. Ashe, *The Discovery of King Arthur*, p. 98.

60. Ashe, *The Discovery of King Arthur*, p. 119.

61. Ashe, *The Discovery of King Arthur*, p. 123.

62. Ashe, *The Discovery of King Arthur*, p. 124.

63. Quoted in Britannia, "King Arthur: Commentary."

Epilogue: Who . . . or What?

64. Quoted in Britannia, "King Arthur: Commentary."

65. William, Chaplain to Bishop Eudo of Leon, "The Legend of St. Goeznovius."

66. Castleden, *King Arthur*, p. 218.

67. Ashe, *The Discovery of King Arthur*, p. 192.

68. William Butler Yeats, "He Wishes for the Cloths of Heaven,"Famous Poems and Poets.

WORKS CONSULTED

Books

Catherine M. Andronik, *Quest for a King*. New York: Atheneum, 1989.

The Anglo-Saxon Chronicles. Trans. Ann Savage. New York: Crescent, 1995.

Geoffrey Ashe, *The Discovery of King Arthur*. New York: Henry Holt, 1985.

Richard Barber, *The Figure of Arthur*. Totowa, NJ: Rowman and Littlefield, 1972.

Rodney Castleden, *King Arthur: The Truth Behind the Legend*. London: Routledge, 2000.

Winston Churchill, *A History of the English-Speaking Peoples*. New York: Dodd, Mead, 1956.

Norma Lorre Goodrich, *King Arthur*. New York: Harper and Row, 1986.

Elizabeth Jenkins, *The Mystery of King Arthur*. New York: Barnes and Noble, 1996.

Jack Lindsay, *Arthur and His Times: Britain in the Dark Ages*. New York: Barnes and Noble, 1966.

Michael O'Neal, ed., *King Arthur: Opposing Viewpoints*. San Diego: Greenhaven, 1992.

Graham Phillips and Martin Keatman, *King Arthur: The True Story*. London: Century Random House, 1992.

Jeremy Roberts, *King Arthur: How History Is Invented*. Minneapolis, MN: Lerner, 2001.

Internet Sources

Annals of Wales (Annales Cambriae), Medieval Sourcebook, Fordham University. www.fordham.edu/halsall/source/annalescambriae.html.

Bede, *The Ecclesiastical History of the English Nation*, Christian Classics Ethereal Library. www.ccel.org/ccel/bede/history.v.html.

Britannia, "King Arthur: Commentary – What the Historians and Writers Say About Him." www.britannia.com/history/arthur/historians.html.

Sheila Brynjulfson, "Geoffrey of Monmouth and the History of the Kings of Britain," Vortigern Studies. www.vortigernstudies.org.uk/artgue/guestsheila3.htm.

Geoffrey of Monmouth, *Arthurian Passages from The History of the Kings of Britain*. Ed. and trans. J.A. Giles. Camelot Project, University of Rochester. www.lib.rochester.edu/Camelot/geofhkb.htm.

Geoffrey of Monmouth, *History of the Kings of Britain*. Trans. Aaron Thompson. Cambridge, ON: In Parentheses, 1999. www.yorku.ca/inpar/geoffrey_thompson.pdf.

Gildas, *Concerning the Ruin of Britain*. Medieval Sourcebook, Fordham University. www.fordham.edu/halsall/source/gildas.html.

Layamon, *Brut*, trans. Eugene Mason, Project Gutenberg. www.gutenberg.org/dirs/1/4/3/0/

14305/14305.txt.

John Leland, *The Itinerary of John Leland, Antiquary*, University of Rochester Camelot Project. www.lib.rochester.edu/camelot/leland.htm.

Linda A. Malcor, "Lucius Artorius Castus, Part 2," *Heroic Age*, no. 2, Autumn/Winter 1999. www.mun.ca/mst/heroicage/issues/2/ha2lac.htm.

Thomas Malory, *Le Morte d'Arthur*, Arthurian Legend. www.arthurian-legend.com/le-morte-darthur/le-morte-darthur-1.php.

Nennius, *Historia Brittonum*, Medieval Sourcebook, Fordham University. www.fordham.edu/halsall/basis/nennius-full.html.

The Quest: An Arthurian Resource, "Sir Mordred the Traitor." www.uidaho.edu/student_orgs/arthurian_legend/knights/orkney/mordred.html#early.

Brian Edward Rise, "Guinevere." *Encyclopedia Mythica*. www.pantheon.org/articles/g/guinevere.html.

University of British Columbia Faculty of Arts, "Guenevere."http://faculty.arts.ubc.casechard/344guen.htm.

Wace, *The "Arthurian" Portions of the Roman de Brut*, trans. Eugene Mason. Cambridge, ON: In Parentheses, 1999. www.yorku.ca/inpar/wace_mason.pdf.

William, Chaplain to Bishop Eudo of Leon, "The Legend of St. Goeznovius," *Britannia: Sources to British History.* www.britannia.com/history/docs/goeznovi.html.

William of Malmesbury, *Chronicle of the Kings of England*, Medieval Sourcebook, Fordham University. www.fordham.edu/halsall/source/malmsbury-chronicle1.html.

William of Newburgh, *The History of William of Newburgh*, Medieval Sourcebook, Fordham University. www.fordham.edu/halsall/basis/williamofnewburgh-one.html#epistle.

William Butler Yeats, "He Wishes for the Cloths of Heaven," Famous Poems and Poets. http://famouspoetsandpoems.com/poets/william_butler_yeats/poems/10175.

For Further Research

Books

Margaret Hodges, *Merlin and the Making of the King*. New York: Holiday House, 2004. Award-winning version of the vast saga of Arthur, nicely condensed and written for younger readers. Beautifully illustrated by Trina Schart Hyman.

Howard Pyle, *King Arthur and His Knights*. West Berlin, NJ: Townsend, 2007. A classic young people's version of the adventures of Arthur and the knights of the Round Table.

Rosemary Sutcliffe, *The Sword and the Circle*. New York: Dutton, 1981. First part of a trilogy that includes *The Light Beyond the Forest* and *The Road to Camlann*. Highly popular version of Arthur's adventures makes a wonderful introduction to the subject for young readers.

Richard White, ed., *King Arthur in Legend and History*. New York: Routledge, 1998. Gathers in one volume all the early documents dealing with King Arthur, including Gildas, the Welsh poems, and the French romances.

Terence Hanbury White, *The Once and Future King*. New York: Putnam, 1958. A brilliant retelling of the Arthurian saga combining four novels written over a period of 20 years—*The Sword in the Stone* (1938), *The Queen of Air and Darkness* (1939), *The Ill-Made Knight* (1940), and *The Candle in the Wind* (1958).

Web Sites

Britannia History: King Arthur (www.britannia.com/history/h12.html). Loads of information in articles about all the major people and places in the Arthurian story. Also has comprehensive guide to other Arthurian Web sites.

The Camelot Project at the University of Rochester (www.lib.rochester.edu/Camelot/cphome.stm). Database of Arthurian texts, images, bibliographies, and basic information sponsored by the University of Rochester and prepared in the Robbins Library.

The Holy Grail (www.boydell.co.uk/www.holygrail.ws/holygrail4.htm). This site, operated by the publisher of Richard Barber's Arthurian books, has a great deal of useful information not directly addressed in the books.

King Arthur: A Man for the Ages (www.geocities.com/CapitolHill/4186/Arthur/html-pages/kingarthur.html). A fun site that seeks to answer such questions as "Was Galahad really so boring?" but also is packed with easy-to-access information.

King Arthur and His Knights of the Round-table (www.kingarthursknights.com). Contains not only information on the story and characters in it, but also has depictions of the characters by artists throughout history.

Index

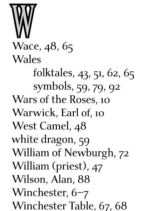

About the Author

William W. Lace is a native of Fort Worth, Texas, where he is executive assistant to the chancellor at Tarrant County College. He holds a bachelor's degree from Texas Christian University, a master's degree from East Texas State University, and a doctorate from the University of North Texas. Prior to joining Tarrant County College, he was director of the News Service at the University of Texas at Arlington and a sportswriter and columnist for the *Fort Worth Star-Telegram*. He has written more than 40 nonfiction books for young readers on subjects ranging from the atomic bomb to the Dallas Cowboys. He and his wife Laura, a retired school librarian, live in Arlington, Texas, and have two children and three grandchildren.